The
Serendipity
of Marriage

REV. DR. JOSEPH D. SMITH

Quantum
Discovery
A LITERARY AGENCY

ISBN
978-1-961601-16-1(Paperback)
978-1-961601-17-8(eBook)

To my beloved wife, Dr. Garnetta Carlton- Smith; our precious daughters, Shreie'e D. Smith and Brionne R. Smith; my siblings; and to all married couples; single men and women; and children.

My mother-in-law the late Mrs. Nellie R. Carlton used a cardboard box approximately 14"x12" in size and turned the cardboard into a church building and she gave it a profound name, Welcome Everybody Baptist Church. She designed the outside and inside to resemble a traditional church building in the 1800 and presented it to me in 1993, during one of her many visits with us.

TABLE OF CONTENTS

PREFACE

I began writing this book on March 31, 2001 around 5:30pm. Earlier on this day, I was sitting in my room and I noticed the brightness of the sun and its warmth, which was a moment of peace and clarity that I was being led by the spirit to write about – why I'm I still married?

Marriage is the union of a man and woman as stated in Genesis 2:24 "Therefore shall a man leave his father and his mother,and shall cleave unto his wife: and they shall be one flesh". There is a combination of thoughts, feelings, a difference in topics of importance as well as various aspects to consider when seeking a mate. As mentioned earlier we will address singles, and those considering remarriage.

Some of the concerns being considered are:

1. Breaking God's commandment
2. Disappointing your significant other; Breaking your spouse's heart even after the "I do's"
3. Confusion with what your children may battle internally and display externally regarding changes in the family dynamics.

The following are steps and acknowledgment of having a healthy, spiritual relationship with God, self and your possible significant other. What would be a great first step, is to own a BIBLE one that you feel comfortable reading and understand. Also, joining a church, attending bible study, of course church service and perhaps being involved in other ministries (service) to fellowship and to gain more knowledge of the bible. Like every story there is a beginning and an end, similar too, some relationships. However, with relationships, until we meet our "soul mate" we need to be ready to work but aware of what work is needed in order to have a long sequence in the relationship versus a short ending. For the never been married singles, it is important to understand that in time you will meet your mate that has been specially prepared for you. You must continue seeking God and busy doing good work in His name. Temptation is in every form, as well as intercourse which is forbidden. As Christians remember that within you carry a temple that you have to labor continually to cast out that sin of man which dwell there in order to corrupt your heart. Leviticus 18:22-23 "Thou shall not lie with mankind, as with womankind: it is abomination. Neither shall you lie with any beast to defile thyself therewith: neither shall any woman stand before a beast to lie down thereto: it is confusion."

"Romans 1:24 & 27 Wherefore, God also gave them up to uncleanness through the lusts of their own hearts, to dishonor their own bodies between themselves: And likewise, also the men, leaving the natural use of the woman, burned in their lust one toward another; men with men working that which is unseemly, and receiving in themselves that recompense of their error which was meet."

To God, you must submit all of yourself to Him, there is no way that God would just take a part of you and be satisfied with it. As you build your relationship with God, you would begin to receive this joy and be glad, with it. There is a dependence that should be established in building your relationship with God. We depend on God and not that He depends on us.

Follow God's Word, we would think at times humanly, only if it's going to give me what I want. It is challenging at times to have the patience and wait on the unknown. When you come on board with God you gain the patience, faith and trust. But if you are not on board with God, it will be more challenging for you to withstand the tide.

Therefore, many people stay away from the relationship with God and just go to the building we call church. God is a spirit, and you need to have God in you and you in Him. That means that you must receive and live by the spirit of God in you.

You get the spirit of God; by first believing in the birth, death and the resurrection of Christ Jesus. As you pray day and night, strengthening your reliance on God through faith, you will slowly start to understand why it was important to establish your first relationship with God before receiving your husband or wife.

So we always hear being equally yoked is important. The words "evenly yoke" means that the man and the woman are in Christ, so when they married they both should have the same interest to continue serving and growing in God. This allows their marriage to benefit from their union with God. The meaning of serendipity is the making of lucky discoveries by chance. (according to who) Webster's.

A great marriage begins with God, which means the man and the woman are spending their life trying to get to know God and His Word. They look to God as the one who will bless their every need.

In our search for a husband or wife we must look at those characteristics of Christ in the man or woman that we meet. Far too often it's only a physical attraction or the performance in the bedroom. The focus on just physique blocks the question on if he or she believes in God and the spiritual side is not considered. Considering a spouse should be given some serious thought.

Maybe at this point in your journey, men you may feel like the ladies you have met do not want to work or they just want to drink and party. Love making; was indirectly for sale if you gave a wedding ring.

And, women the men you have met are lazy, low down, fast or slick talking, just game and just wanted to have intercourse with any female.

So now you must evaluate and process what type of man, or woman should I be looking for? I need to find someone, quickly, my body, mind, and soul is in much pain for love. The example for what you should be; looking for in a man or woman is right in your home or in the bible. Your parents, if they are followers of Christ, look to them for answers to some of your questions, with God direction.

Too, much time is spent on acquiring material items, worldly possessions, and not enough time spent serving God, to be directed to finding that husband or wife.

The husband is in the image of Christ Jesus, and the wife represent, the church. Jesus, shed His blood for the church (all the people in the world) and when He comes again: He will be coming for the church (those that are Following Him)

God can supply all our needs and allow us to have our wants.

Chapter 1

Relationships

Serving God should not be a chore, but a delight to place you at His feet of mercy to gain the understanding of His Word. This thought came to me about my personal relationship with God. Although at times it seems hard, I am working daily on enjoying and trusting what God has for me. I know God has blessed me with a great deal of things but there are so many other things that are going on in my head that I don't always understand. I'm thankful that the Grace's were patient with me when they were trying to take me to church. I mean I was upset with God on how he could let my biological parents give me up and I had to bounce from home to home. I'm innocent going through so much pain and what felt like rejection. I never understood why my parents didn't think about keeping me instead of giving me up at three months. After going from home to home I was finally adopted at the age of eight.

I enjoy living with the Grace family, growing up with their children, as my siblings, and just being accepted by them. I have mixed feelings at times about trust, relationships, especially my role of a big brother and oh yeah, girls and dating them. Both Mr. and Mrs. Grace are nice people who have been helping and encouraging me through my rough times. Especially when I'm going through my moments feeling down, empty or not able to make it due to not knowing my biological parents, what they were like or if I even have anymore siblings, just not knowing my biological family, who is a part of me.

I struggle with this even more since I have gotten older, wanting to ask questions to my biological parents, but I know God knows how I feel and I guess I shouldn't worry about it because of being placed with the Grace's, which was God's plan. So speaking of planning, both Mr. and Mrs. Grace want me to go off to college, do well for myself and overall they just want the best for me. After watching some of my favorite television shows with police action and charismatic attorneys making changes, I've been considering becoming a lawyer. That way, as a lawyer I believe I can help people and do something good in the community. Funny, where we can get our inspirations, right? I'm excited and all of this sounds great, I have been looking at colleges, but I've also been seeing someone. The Grace's know about Beth and they want me to be careful with her that I don't make decisions or do anything that will take me off the plan of going to college. I am going to college, but I'm just concerned about what is going to happen to us with the separation. I mean Beth wants to go to New York University and I've heard that those New York guys are real slick with playing games with the ladies. I know that there are some unreasonable things that guy's do to females, I am not saying that it is right, it part of the game.

Beth and I have talked about the different colleges that we plan to attend, but to be truthful I am not sure about the distance. Plus I don't want this type of stress of thinking that Beth could be with someone else, other than me. I know that Beth and I need to talk about the different colleges we are planning to attend and the distance that will be between us.

I know that I have been seeing Beth for a while and I start thinking that because my parents gave me up I don't want to give up Beth. I know the situation is different, but the feeling of being separated from someone close is still there. I really don't know how I would feel if Beth went away from me.

I'm thinking, now that maybe the best thing for us to do is to remain close to each other while attending college. Let me find out if Beth have been thinking about this distant for us while we are at college. Hi, Beth, what are your thoughts about college for us if I am going to Yale University and your at New York University. What are we going to do about that? Because, there are some real slick guys there, wait Jerry I know that you think that because I am going to New York.

We have a history together, and all that we mean to one another was just a waste of time. You see that's the way that guy's think. And I am not going to let you off the hook that easy you said that you cared for me I didn't twist your arm to have you say those word so don't come out of that type of bag with me. No, no, no, Beth that's not the reason why I said what

I did? Oh, let me go home and think about this and finger out something that would help us through this mess that I brought up.

Beth don't gave up on me, yes, I care for you don't throw me out because of what I just said. I'll call you to explain what we can do about this distant that we have with college. Bob, shouted, hey Jerry what's wrong? Dose, Beth have you tied to her apron string. Jerry looked at Bob as he passed by in the car that John was driving and knew that he did not like Bob's sarcastic comment. Well I think I need to taken in a movie; what do you think Beth? Do you think, that we will be okay,I need to check with my father. Okay, how about seven o'clock, and I will see if my father will let me us the car. Well, if I listen to what Bob is saying about me tired to Beth apron that really makes me feel like I can not think on my own without Beth, and that is not right for Bob to say that at all. After all, his father, is an alcoholic, and he beats everyone in the family. But, I really shouldn't feel that way because he has that type of problem in the family that he need to work through every day. Okay, that's enough of being down because of what some one has said about me, I need to take care of my work at home before my father and mother gets home. Pauline, Michael, and Franklin will be home any minute now and things need to be clean by the time that mother and father arrives home. Hi, Jerry, hi, guys, every one knows what they need to do before father and mother get home. Pauline are you still talking, yes Jerry and I am on my way to my bedroom, then I'll clean the bonus room up from you guys messing up the room. You should have clean this room up since the three of you played your games last night.

Michael how's the clearing going with the living room? Jerry, most of the room is finish I just need to dust a little and every thing would be done. Franklin, I done hear any thing, what are you doing now: sleeping, no, Jerry I just wanted to check on some thing in my bedroom, than I will be right down. No, Franklin, you need to do your chores first, then you can go and do: what every you need to, later? Come on Franklin, Okay Jerry hear I come. Michael, you know that there are reasons why we just don't agree on many things, that's because I know it all and you are trying to be as smart as I am.

Okay, Pauline: If you're so smart; why dose it say in the bible, women need to listen to their husband. No, your wrong Michael, you need to show that to me in the bible. Look Pauline just because you don't like the discussion it doesn't mean that the information is wrong. A lot of time has gone into research of the bible and they have found that it is correct with these statements that have been made. So it is important for each of us to do research before we argue our point of view.

Anyway Pauline what is with the bus stop? The bus stop you know that mother told you about, that you should come right home. But, Jerry, that's okay you and Michael can say all that you want to, I am much old now than I was two years ago. Anyhow, I am going to talk to mother about the reason I was at the bus stop this time I am sure she would understand. All right, I don't know what is going on: has every one finish their chores? Pauline said, hi mother and dad, mother is it all right now for me to get off the bus where Michael and Franklin get off? No, Pauline I though you understood what I was talking about years ago? What happen this time Pauline? Will, there's this boy and I like him, can we talk in the living about this mother without, everyone looking at me. The, everyone is your family Pauline and they will know what is going on: No I just, right now want to talk to you mother okay. Excuse me Paul let me see what is on Pauline mine, so that there can be some understanding to this mystery that Pauline don't want every one to hear. Okay, Pauline what's up? Well, this boy his nice, and I road on the bus to the stop where Michael and Franklin get off the bus, because he lives in that area of the neighborhood.

Okay, this boy, what his name, Larry, you got off the bus at your brothers bus stop because you wanted to ride on the bus with some boy name Larry. Oh, he nice, mother, wait Pauline I never told you that it was okay for you to start seeing boys, have I? No, but I though that it would be find. There are many things that you may want to do, but let me explain some things to you.

It is not easy for female and you need to make sure that you are not moving to fast with any young man that may interrupt your future plans with your education. That is the reason for your father and I are spending a great deal of time with you and your brothers in the church, so you would be better prepared in order to handle this situation. You can't spend to much time in the Word of God, because the more that you study the word the more wisdom you receive.

Pauline don't think that you are exempt from any thing happening to you from any boy. We are seeking wisdom so that you can know that this is not good right now for you and it may be to difficult at this moment to understand. Jerry, how can you help your sister to understand what I am saying right now. Pauline mother is telling you the right things there are three girls in my classroom that are pregnant.

Well, mother I plan to take Beth to the movies; I need to leave now in order that I will not miss the start of the movie. Mr. Reynolds, is Beth only parent and I know that it must be hard on her not having a mother to talk with, because her father is going to do only the things that he is a were of from a man's point of view. I am sure that's difference from what her mother would do? All we know are problems, and I know there is a word in the bible about what single people should be doing, let me find this before I leave to pick Beth up. Oh, here it is let me read this to better understand.

Unmarried People-I Corinthians 7:8-9 "I say therefore to the unmarried and widows, It is good for them if they abide even as I. But if they cannot contain, let them marry: for it is better to marry than to burn."

concerning virgins I have no commandment of the Lord.

Yet I give my judgment, as one that hath obtained mercy of the Lord to be faithful. I suppose therefore that this is good for the present distress, I say, that it is good for a man so to be. Art they bound unto a wife? Seek not to be loosed. Art thou loosed from a wife? Seek not a wife. But and if thou marry, thou hast not sinned; and if a virgin marry, she hath not sinned. Nevertheless such shall have trouble in the flesh: but I spare you.

But this I say brethren, the time is short: it remain that both they that have wives be as though they had none. And they that weep, as though they wept not; and they that rejoiced not; and they that buy, as though they possessed not. And, they that use this world, as not abusing it: for the fashion of this world passeth away.

But I would have you without carefulness. He that is unmarried careth for the things that belong to the Lord, how he may please the Lord: But he that is married careth for the things that are of the world, how he may please his wife.

There is a difference also between a wife and a Virgin. The unmarried woman careth for the things of the Lord, that she may be holy both in body and in spirit: but she that is married careth for the things of the world, how she may please her husband.

And this I speak for your own profit; not that I may cast a snare upon you, but for they which is comely, and that ye may attend upon the Lord without distraction. But if any man think that he behaveth himself uncomely toward his virgin, if she pass the flower of her age, and need so require, let him do what he will, he sinneth not: let them marry.

Never the less he that standeth stedfast in his heart, having no necessity, but hath power over his own will, and have so decreed in his heart that he will keep his virgin, doeth well. So then he that giveth her in marriage doeth well; but he that giveth her not in marriage doeth better.

The wife is bound by the law as long as her husband live; but if her husband be dead, she is at liberty to be married to whom ever she will; only in the Lord. But she is happier if she so abide, after my judgment; and I think also that I have the Spirit of God."

Now, I still have questions about the marriage thing, I guess I really need to know how do you know when you have found the right person to marry. Look I know that there are many difference types of family structure and who has the best structure of all.

There are families with just the mother and the children; there are families with the father and children: there are families where children are adopted; and there are families that have two females; and there are families with two males and there are families that have a father and mother.

I am not trying to be better but I do like the fact that I have a father. Some one that can help me to understand things from the male view point and letting me know how you should treat females. On the other hand I am glad that I have a mother, who will let me know things about females that I need to be watch for of.

Receiving love and the mental strength from your mother and father helps to balance many things in your life. There is a lot to learn as a young adult about the oppose sex and most of that information is in secret code, until your able to intersect some of the passing of the code, to understand it, in order to use it, to your advantage.

Will dad and mother I really need to go and pick up Beth if we are going to see this move tonight. Okay, Jerry, be safe, tell Mr. Reynolds that we send our love to him. I will tell him mother, go by.

Oh, what time is it? Man I did plan to send that much time in the house with the family but it is always nice to do that with them because they are my parents that I know and they care for me.

Beth, hi I am sorry for running a little late but I got tried up with my family and I wanted to read this scripture to give me some understanding as a single person. Mr. Reynolds, my parents told me to tell you hell-o. Thanks Jerry, tell you parents the same to them. Okay, we better go Beth, Jerry, are you okay with everything about college?

Beth, I should have said something to my parents on how we are having a hard time with this distant between school, but I'll talk to them later.

Okay, were here, Jerry don't said any thing to John or Bob, Hey look who is hear it the guys, well Jerry I see, that you are out I guess that mean that you guys are okay with the kids.

Look, Bob, I just wanted to see a movies with Beth not hear a lot of lip from you or John. Is it all right with you guys if we get seat inside, thank you?

The movies, was good and long it was the Princes, the girls spent most of they time drying their eyes throughout the movies. The guys like the character; that played on the girls in the movies, that's what Bob and John liked.

Now that the movie was over, and we all walked back to our cars, we were very silence. That guy, who Chat, John said, he was bad with the ladies: Oh no. You think he was something; he was sometime great, you want to be like him. Then go right ahead Bob, I won't be with you.

Susan what is wrong? Did I upset you, because I said how I liked the character in the movies: yes, Bob I know deep down inside that is how you really wanted to act. Look Bob, why don't you just quite talking like that to Susan. Hey Jerry I know who I am talking to, and Susan knows mean. Okay Susan and Jane there isn't any reason for the two of you to upset yourselves over some movies. Beth, I know that you right. Your know I don't want to think that Bob wanted to be like Chat but for some reason he may need to get someone else; to jerk around and it's not going to be me.

Are you going to let them take you home? Or, do you want Jerry to bring you home. Oh yet. So you can say all that you want to say Susan. But, if you keep that up, I guess you'll walk home. What are you talking about Bob? I am not walking home, and if you think that you can be by yourself; just don't call me. Fine Susan. I won't call you. I am going to the car Susan, if you want a ride home, with me lets go John and Jane. Come on, come on, Susan Bob really didn't mean those things.

Yes, he did Jane. I'm hurt right now. I want an apology from Bob. Bob, said I'll see you. Beth did you see that! Bob just pulled out of the parking lot; and sped up down the street.

Jerry, you need to talk with Bob, right now; you need to give Susan a ride home, okay Susan lets go to the car. Susan, I know that you're upset with Bob and I understand that, but don't let that get you down about everything, may be Jerry can talk with Bob tomorrow. Beth I don't think Susan heard a word that you where saying to her because she is to upset, to respond to you right now.

Jerry, I guess this is going to be a quiet ride. Let me turn on some music to keep my spirit up beat about every thing. Okay Jerry if you turn right then left Susan house will be on the right the second house. Beth said okay Susan we are here, Jerry while don't you walk with us to the door. Susan do you have your house key? Yes, Beth I have the key and I thank you and Jerry for bring me home I don't know what I' am going to do? I will call you Susan and talk then, right now why don't you go and get some rest, do you want a hug? Susan, said yes Beth, oh, excuse me for cry on you. Susan I know the feeling that you have for Bob the tears are okay so dry your eyes, and by morning most of this pain, would have gone away.

Wow! Gee! What is wrong? I wanted to take in a movie, but I didn't think that this would have happened to them. I know that Bob, wants to do what every it is that Bob wants to do. But I just didn't think that he would do that to Susan.

He just took off and left Susan, to get home the best way that she could; ten miles away from home. Jerry, that was bad and you need to talk to Bob. About what happened and about, what he did tonight? You know Beth this is making me think about our relationship. What do you mean? Make you think; No, don't get me wrong. Beth this is not negative, it just let me know the important, of respect that should be displayed for each other at all time.

You need to call Susan, and talk to her, because she should not have gotten herself worked up over that movie. About what Bob said. We have a long ways to go. I guess we need to spend more time, talking to our parents;

to find out, how have they been able to stay together all these years. What is the missing pieces to the puzzle?

You know Beth this is something to really think about for us. Well, Jerry we always need to gain a deeper understanding about the things that are going on around us every single daily, because it can effect your spirit. You know I just, want think right now, enough to see what I really want. You know that was a nice quite ride to your house, I guess I wasn't the only one in deep though about things. Okay, Beth we are at the house. Beth, why did you grabbed my arm? Wait Jerry: Do you like me yes or no?

Beth you know that I do. No Jerry, answer my question, yes Beth I like you.

Look you know that we need to get out this car before your father think that there is something going on in here. I don't want to be in any trouble with your father Beth. Let's go Beth, okay, this is nice Jerry holding hands as you walk me to the door. Beth, I want to kiss you, Oh, my father is at the door. Oh, Mr. Reynolds, yes did you two enjoy the movies? Yes sir, we did. Well, I guess I will be on my way home. Oh, Jerry gave me a hug. Well, good night, Mr. Reynolds and good night Beth. I'll call you tomorrow.

Oh, yea, I need to stop at the gas station, in order to get some gas, for my dad car before I arriving home.

I wonder why the lights were still on, in the house. Let me put the car in the garage and find out what is going on with dad and mother, for them to still be up on a Friday night. After opening the garage door and driving the car inside the garage, he let the garage door down and got out of the car and walk to the door, of the house.

Let me find the key, oh, hi Dad, what's wrong? What's wrong? Your mother told me about Pauline why didn't you say something when your mother and I arrived home from work.

Well, I was going to say something, but I did tell you both about Pauline getting off the bus and coming home with Michael. No, no that's not what we are talking about; who is this boy named Larry? Larry! Who is he? Well, that's what we are asking you, Jerry?

Well! I don't know who Larry is dad and mother. So that's the reason why Pauline got off the bus, not to come home with Michael and Franklin. I bet that conversion they were having was just a smoke screen, on why she real got off the bus.

Dad, Mom, did either of you asked Michael if he knew Larry? No not yet, we just wanted to speak to you to find out what you knew about this boy. Well son: how did you and Beth enjoy the movie? The movies, was nice, but the things that happen between Bob and Susan it wasn't nice at all. Bob just left Susan standing there upset. What? What's wrong with Bob leaving Susan that far away from home? Well, who did Susan, go home with?

I took her home dad. I think you for doing that.

Wait, Jerry did any one call Susan parents or Bob parents about this incident. No, well I think. Mother I told you about their problem but not for you to call Susan's parents.

I am not trying to start anything, no it's not going to be anything, trust me. See dad can you talk to mother, for her not to call over Bob or Susan house. I am going to talk to Bob tomorrow and if things don't go well, mother can call their parents. Okay Dad?

Okay Jerry. I'll ask your mother to give you a chance to work thing out with Bob and Susan. I know that you'll need a few days for this okay. Okay dad thinks. Oh dad, I have a question. How come; you and mother remain together for so long and Mr. and Mrs. Right?

What makes some people stay together, when many others people are getting divorce? And why is there fornication, adultery, men with men and women with women?

Chapter 2

Learning to Live by God's Word

Look Jerry, there are many things in life that I will never have the answers to, but I have leaned over the years; that God has the answers to all of our questions, and he holds the keys to life and death.

Okay, so when can you explain to me the answer to the questions that I just asked? Look Jerry, you been in bible class, Sunday school and in the church for a long time we brought you and your brothers and sister up in the church. Have you listen to the pastor as he is preaching his sermon. Yes, but I don't recall any sermon on the question that I am asking.

Look Jerry. Okay, after we get up tomorrow: and you return from over Bob house. We will have some discussion on the subjects. I'll tell your brothers, sister, and your mother about the class session.

I want to give you a hug for that and good night dad. You know I need to go down this hallway to tell mother good night. Mother, come in Jerry I just stopped in to give you a hug and kiss. Oh that was nice Jerry, good night mother; Good night Jerry.

I know that the bible tells me that we need to pray for our family and friends. Lord, watch over Beth, Bob, Susan, John, Jane and my family Amend.

Man I must have slept very hard last night because I didn't hear anything at all, But now I know what I need to do this day once I get things done around the house. That's right, I did tell Beth that I would have away for us to be able to cope with this long distance.

Hey, Franklin, do you want to play some games in the hallway let's go, hey, Michael be careful don't hit the wall you're going to wait up father and mother. Mother! will you please tell Michael and Franklin to stop playing around, in the hall. Some of us want to sleep, like me!

Look Pauline, why did you feel the need to raise your voice and call me, having me get up? Why didn't you just ask your brothers to stop playing in the hallway; or for them to just go to their rooms? Now since you got me up: Now we will get up and have breakfast early, do our chores and some other things. Hay, we are going to do some bible study, after everyone complete their chores. Oh Michael, you and Franklin; one of you get in the bathroom, and then let the other one know when you're out of the bathroom, before you get dress.

Paul, I real love you, well come on over here girl; no you see every time, I tell you something, you get the wrong ideal. Wrong ideal! Me no Diane. Then what did you mean by your statement, wrong ideal Paul, you got to make it quick, well come over here.

Hey, Franklin it's your turn to go into the bathroom and hurry up so we can finish playing. Oh don't forget to tell Pauline, when you come out of the bathroom. This really upset me because I had to get up, when Michael and Franklin were playing in the hallway not me. I all ways get the short end because of my brothers. I'll fit them the next time and mother will not need to take their side. I should be the last one going in the bathroom not Jerry I am the only girl in the family and I should have rights to do some special things as a female. Okay, Jerry, I am out of the bathroom Prince your tub away you, get up Jerry, if I can't sleep than you won't sleep.

Since I told Jerry to go in the bathroom I guess I can take my time going down stairs to the kitchen. I finish getting dress and come down the stairs when Jerry comes out of his bedroom.

Good morning Jerry, good morning Pauline: Why are you pushing on me Pauline? I didn't tell you to get up, you did that on your own, with your big mouth, that messed everything up for every one. Stop! Speed it up here, let go! let go!

Thank you, Paul for setting the table and getting the milk and orange juice. Franklin would you check the front porch for the newspaper. Pauline I didn't have anything to do with; what happen to you on yesterday? So stop! I am going to push you back, and I know that; your not going to like it!

Pauline, if you hit Jerry, then I am going to hit you, but mother, he, he did what Pauline. Remember you got off the bus. Let's eat, all right every one bow their head, Lord, bless this food that you have made available by giving us jobs and strength, Lord help us to keep our focus on you and bless the hands that have prepared the food, I ask these blessing in your son Jesus name. Amen.

I am hungry and this food is good mother, yes it is Diane. Mother, what are going to do after, breakfast? Well, Pauline we must complete the chores around the house and your father already said that we are going to have bible study once everyone complete their chores.

Mother, dose that mean that I need to wash the dishes or is it Pauline turn? Well that's a fair question Jerry, Pauline I think it is time for you to start cleaning the kitchen: Do a good job Pauline. Mother that's not fair Jerry always. Never mind mother I'll do the dish.

Look every one we should be able to finish or chores within the hour. Would that be fair to everyone?

Now, before I begin; I wanted everyone to have their own bible. So, that we all can read the same printed scripture.

Now where do we begin? Why not just start with the subjects that I said last night?

Okay, so you're the one that prompted this bible study. What's your problem Jerry? Beth is looking at someone else. Pauline, if you cannot control yourself I'll give you sometime out, that will help you remember who you need to respect at all times. Okay, mother.

Okay, let's start at the beginning in Genesis chapter one; but why are we starting there dad, because it is important to understand creation and God's command, on human relationship.

Spiritual, relationship should be develop with God, to make earthly relationship more meaningful and loving. Yes, we all have a role to play and our responsibilities are outlined for men and women. Rules are important for us to fellow: what the bible tells us, and not to use the bible just to try, to strengthen out other people.

We don't look at the whole bible as a guide to live by, or a tool to correct our behavior, or to correct our views on how life could be if we live by the

Word of God. So now Genesis Chapter one said, "In the beginning God created the heaven and the earth. And the earth was without form, and void; and darkness was upon the face of the deep.

And the spirit of God moved upon the face of the waters.

And God said, let there be light: and there was light. And God saw the light, that it was good: and God divided the light from the darkness. And God called the light day, and the darkness he called night.

And the evening and the morning were the first day.

And God said, let there be a firmament in the midst of the waters, and let it divide the waters from the waters. And God made the firmament, and divided the waters which were under the firmament from the waters which were above the firmament: and it was so. And God called the firmament heaven. And the evening and the morning were the second day.

And God said, let the waters under the heaven be gathered together unto one place, and let the dry land appear: And it was so. And God called the dry land earth; And the gathering together of the waters called he Seas: And God saw that it was good. And God said, let the earth bring forth grass, the herb yielding fruit after his kind, and whose seed is in itself, upon the earth: and it was so.

And the earth brought forth grass, and herb yielding seed after his kind, and the tree yielding fruit whose seed was in itself, after his kind: and God saw that it was good.

And the evening and the morning were the third day. And God said, let there be lights in the firmament of the heaven to divide the day from the night; and let them be for signs, and for seasons, and for days, and years;

And let them be for lights in the firmament of the heaven to give light upon the earth: and it was so. And God made two great lights; the greater light to rule the day, and the lesser light to rule the night: he made the stars also. And God set them in the firmament of the heaven to give light upon the earth; And to rule over the day and over the night, and to divide the light from the darkness: and God saw that it was good.

And the evening and the morning were the fourth day. And God said, let fowl that may fly above the earth in the open firmament of heaven. And God created great whales, and every living creature that move, which the waters brought forth abound; after their kind and every winged fowl after his kind: and God saw it was good.

And God blessed them, saying, be fruitful, and multiply, and fill the water in the seas, and let fowl multiply in the earth. And the evening and the morning were the fifth day. And God said, let the earth bring forth the living creature after his kind, cattle, and creeping thing, and beast of the earth after his kind: and it was so.

And God made the beast of the earth after his kind; and cattle after their kind, and every thing that creep upon the earth after his kind: and God saw that it was good. And God said, let us make man in our image, after our likeness: and let them have dominion over the fish of the Sea, and over the fowl of the air, and over the cattle, and over all the earth, and over every creeping thing that creep upon the earth.

So God created man in his own image, in the image of God created he him; male and female created he them. And God blessed them, and God said unto them, be fruitful, and multiply, and replenish the earth, and subdue it: and have dominion over the fish of the sea, and over the fowl of the air, and over every living thing that move upon the earth.

And God said, behold, I have given you every herb bearing seed, which is upon the face of all the earth, and every tree, in the which is the fruit of a tree yielding seed; to you it shall be for meat. And to every beast of the earth, and to every fowl of the air, and to every thing that creepe upon the earth, wherein there is life, I have given every green herb for meat: and it was so.

And God saw every thing that he had made, and, behold, it was very good. And the evening and the morning were the sixth day."

Oh wow, dad, God is powerful, He made everything, then why are we in bad shape? Everything was perfect. Dose God, see everything and knows what we are thinking? Yes, Pauline he knows it all so pray to Him.

You see we start doing thing very early in life and continue to create more things that are sinful to us. This scripture tells us when we start speaking untruthfully.

In Psalm 58:3 said, "The wicked are estranged from the womb: they go astray as soon as they are born, speaking lies."

So, what chance do we have to make it into heaven? Look, we all have a chance to make it into heaven; that's the reason why it is so importance to study the Word of God, the bible. Wait, you just read that "God created man in his own image, in the image of God created he, him; male and female" is that the reason that there are grays people and lesbian people, no son. God has given the man the ability to give his wife the seed of a boy or girl according to his blessing to the husband and his wife.

You see, God allowed us to make choices and this scripture tells us how we are" Chosen to live a Holy Life-I Peter 1:13-25 Wherefore gird up the loins of your mind, be sober, and hope to the end for the grace that is to be brought unto you at the revelation of Jesus Christ; As obedient children, not fashioning yourselves according to the former lusts in your ignorance:

But as he which has called you is holy, so be you holy in all manner of conversation; Because; it is written, Be you holy; for I am holy. And if you call on the Father, who without respect of persons judge according to every man's work, pass the time of your sojourning here in fear: For as much as you know that ye were not redeemed with corruptible things, as silver and gold, from your vain conversation received by tradition from your father;

But with the precious blood of Christ, as of a lamb without blemish and without spot: Who verily was foreordained before the foundation of the world, but was manifest in these last times for you. Who by him do believe in God; that raised him up from the dead, and gave him glory; that your faith and hope might be in God.

Seeing you have purified your souls in obeying the truth through the Spirit unto unfeigned love of the brethren, see that you love one another with a pure heart fervently. Being born again, not of corruptible seed, but of incorruptible, by the word of God, which live and abideth for ever.

For all flesh is as grass, and all the glory of man as the flower of grass. The grass withereth, and the flower thereof falleth away: But the word of the Lord endure for ever. And this is the word which by the gospel is preached unto you."

So, gray people are committing a sin then? Yes, Jerry, their act is sinful and we will get into it, not today later here or in bible study. One of the things you must keep in mine. As, I said, earlier we need to study the bible to correct ourselves, but we are always trying to correct other people. We should find out how we can "Please others and not yourself-Romans 15:1-6 We then that are strong ought to bear the infirmities of the weak, and not to please ourselves, Let every one of us please his neighbour for his good to edification. For even Christ pleased not himself; but as it is written.

The reproaches of them that reproached thee fell on me.

For whatsoever things were written aforetime were written for our learning, that we through patience and comfort of the scriptures might have hope. Now the God of patience and consolation grant you to be likeminded one toward another according to Christ Jesus: That you may with one mind and one mouth glorify God, even the Father of our Lord Jesus Christ."

Now, if, we apply the Word of God to our life, then as, I am telling you now, you will be more loving to each other and more obedient to your mother and I. When you apply God's principle to your daily living, many problems, can just melt away. Because God allows you to see, the beauty and the benefit in each thing that has happen to you, to strengthen you spiritually, with your faith walk, with Him. So we need rules to guide us to make sure that we are doing the right thing as best that we can so "Rules for Christian Living- Romans 12:9-21 Let love be without dissimulation. Abhor that which is evil; cleave to that which is good. Be kindly affectioned one to another with brotherly love; in honour preferring one another; Not slothful in business; fervent in spirit; serving the Lord; Rejoicing in hope; patient in tribulation; continuing instant in prayer;

Distributing to the necessity of saints; given to hospitality. Bless them, which persecute you: bless, and curse not. Rejoice with them that do rejoice, and weep with them that weep. Be of the same mind one toward another. Mind not high things, but condescend to men of low estate. Be not wise in your own conceits.

Recompense to no man evil for evil. Provide things honest in the sight of all men. If it be possible, as much as lieth in you, live peaceably with all men. Dearly beloved, avenge not yourselves, but rather give place unto wrath: for it is written, Vengeance is mine; I will repay, saith the Lord.

Therefore if thine enemy hunger, feed him; if he thirst, give him drink: for in so doing thou shalt heap coals of fire on his head. Be not overcome of evil, but overcome evil with good."

And that is; because you place God, at the forefront in everything you do, and thank God to direct you; and to truly receive his mercy that you have humble yourself before him, to do the will of God. And just not when it is to benefit you only.

Now! I want all of you to do this: What dad? I know that we have spent a little time in chapter one of Genesis. Okay, Dad, maybe I didn't listen to the teachers, in Sunday school or bible class; but just now: It is like my eyes are opened from what you just said dad. I want to be strong, and understand were my strength come from, and know that: One day I can be in love, and know that I can still love; that lady just like you, and mother are in love many years later.

So many things are going on, but I want to, okay Jerry, it's not a one sided relationship, you must be willing to turn your life over to God. And that young lady that you wish to married must also, turned her life over to God; to make your earthly relationship work even with problems. You must learn to believe, have faith in God, keep your dreams a live, and always pray at good time or when things are difficult.

Well it's not easy, Jerry, your father and I didn't have a relationship with God until after we were married.

However, we are trying to correct you, Pauline, Michael, and Franklin so that you can have that relationship, with God early to enjoy life blessing at a young age.

Jerry, I know you heard guys complain about girl's attitude, and some of the problems that females have; because of nature and some are just them. God's wisdom, when you have that relationship, with God, you can understand the nature side, and the phony side. Which will let you know: that she is not for real or he is not for real.

And for you Pauline, even though you are not Jerry's age, there are some boy's that you're sick of; because of their attitude. Well the same think applies to you just as I stated to Jerry. You need God, in your life. Michael and Franklin, there is no escape for you, you need God not to look at girls, but to know how to treat girls, nice, and treating all people with love and kindness. Now this is a scripture that I want to read to everyone:

"Faith and Wisdom- James 1:2-8 My brethren, count it all joy when ye fall into divers temptations; Knowing this, that the trying of yout faith worketh patience. But let patience have her perfect work, that ye may be perfect and entire, wanting nothing, If any of you lack wisdom, let him ask of God, that giveth to all men liberally, and upbraideth not; and it shall be given him.

But let him ask in faith, nothing wavering. For he that wavereth is like a wave of the sea driven with the wind and tossed. For let not that man think that he shall receive any thing of the Lord. A double-minded man is unstable in all his ways."

Will I guess your mother covered the other part that was needed and it does not matter what you do; to do it right with understanding, you need God, in your life, and in your plans.

Listen; tomorrow at church I want all of you to understand: What the pastor is preaching about? Rev. Dr. Johnson is telling everyone about God's goodness, and God's rapture.

Now; we are all members of "Welcome Everybody Baptist Church". And because, we are studying the Word of God: we must show everyone who we speak with, how we conduct ourselves, because of how the Word of God is within us. Remember God sent His only Son to die for us, Jesus Christ, and He rose on the third day; with all power in His hand.

All right Mother, I am thinking about our discussion in reference to Larry and now; with all this information today about everything; am I to become a nun? May be that is what it will take; for now, until your on your way to college. Okay, mother I heard you the first time and I understood all that you have said. Dad, I'll run to the store to pick up those items that you and mother need and will stop over to Bob's on my way back home.

By the time that, I make it over to Bob's house it was about 1:30 P.M. Now, I don't think that I'll be over here to long, hopefully Bob has cool down and have come to his sense. Oh, man, why is Bob walking around like he is lost and talking to himself. Hey, Bob, hi Jerry, hey man how are you doing, okay, Bob.

Why? What's wrong Bob? Why are you looking loss? Look, Jer, Susan mother called my parents this morning, because I left her, man you got to help me out, or, or what Bob? You left Susan to prove what point, no man you got it all wrong, you see. I was just testing her.

Well did you go back to see if she got home all right, no, but I knew you were going to cover for me, Jer.

Wait, Bob, you want me to tell your parents what?

And you never went back to see if Susan was okay or called her at all. What is going on Bob? If you don't, tell my parents that you have my back. I cannot go anywhere or drive my car for the next two months. Hey, man you got to help me out bro.

Chapter 3

The Need of A Loving Relationship with God

Look Bob, I don't want you, to be grounded for the next two months, but you know your parents, and you know what you did. Last night was dumb or stupid, yea, yea your right Jer, so, will you cover may back man. You see, I got to call Susan, to smooth this thing out with her.

Wait, Bob, smooth this thing out, do you understand what you did! You took off and left her ten miles from home, in front, of a theater. I don't think your going to smooth anything out, or smooth over things, with Susan the way she was upset last night.

I think you, may need to get, on your hands and knees, and then may be; Susan may listen to you. Look Jer, just because you do that with Beth, don't think I, Bob, is going to do that with Susan. She know who I am, and that's that, look Bob, look man, all I want you to due, is to tell my parents, our low down, okay, you got that Jer, no, Bob, I don't have it.

Maybe you have my low down. You deal with your parents, and have your parents cover your back, see ya later Bob. You just wait one minute Jer, I am the man, and Susan can't tell me anything. Hey Bob, I'll see you, at church tomorrow, by.

Well, I guess that when really great. Now Bob, is acting like a jerk, he just didn't want to listen to anyone I had to say.

Now, let me go over to Beth may be she had better luck talking to Susan, than what I had with Bob.

I guess I'll drive through town it's a shorter rout to Beth house. Oh, what is this, a group of gray guys, and lesbian ladies walking in the down

20

town area. I wonder what they are up to this time. Hey, I think I know them: would you like to meet me at church tomorrow; I was surprise when they said Yes. Oh, Jerry, don't think that we are going to change. I believe when you hear the message it will be the reason for your change of mind. What we do is not in the bible or is it a sin? Okay what time Jerry, 11:00 A.M. morning service!

I finally made it over to Beth house, and told her about Bob's attitude: also I met some people that I knew; and I invited them to church. Don't you think the church is going to be in an uproar!

Well, Beth, the church is for all people, even you and I need to understand more about God's wonder just to start building a relationship, with Him. Well, I guess your right Jerry. So is Bob going to be there; I think so, he's been grounded for two months and he will be attend church, with his parents.

Susan, and I talked about last night and she appears to be feeling better today and was wondering if she would see Bob at church tomorrow, to tell him a piece of her mind. Susan also told me that Jane called to see how she was doing, and John was sorry about what went on last night between, she and Bob.

Hi Mr. Reynolds, hi Jerry, I see that your father is doing some lawn work. Well Beth, I knew that there was still a need to talk, about our feelings. What do we need to talk about?

It's a lot to think about and still try to remain focus on each other?

But, you see Beth, if we lean on God, the stronger our faith become, and the more we study God's Word, life becomes clear as we learn and grow. We must study our bibles more, to accept God and His Word each day.

Beth, I just want a hug right now. Beth, I'll call you later on tonight or I'll see you in church. No, you call me tonight, and I'll see you at church tomorrow.

He is God and holds all power in His hands, and because of our sins; Jesus died for us, and we think that; we can be like a god.

Sometime the days just come quicker then you think and Sunday morning is here and my family is up and we are getting ready for church. We ate cereal and toast as we rushed out the door for Sunday school at 9:30 A.M. We made it to church and then went to our assigned classes.

After Sunday school, we had the Sunday school lesson review, and than started walking to the sanctuary for the morning service.

I know that it has been hard on Beth with one parent after loosen her mother three years ago. I am sure, her father have deep memories about Mrs. Reynolds because of his love he had for her. And now Beth he must rise by himself. Many things that Beth, mother have told her I guess the next door neighbor helps to answer questions that Beth may want to discuss. I can just image the pain that Beth must be in not having her mother with her at this moment and time of getting ready to go off to college.

I also, know that I can not be playing with Beth feeling about our relationship if I am not in it for us.

I see my family; mother and dad are going to the front of the church. Let me talk to my parents, dad and mother, I need to talk to you, about something after service today, would you have time this evening. What is this about? Is Beth, Jerry, quickly said no, dad and mother, Beth is not. Okay, but why do you want to talk to us.

Because, you are going to tell me the truth, to the questions, I need answers to. Okay, right after we eat and the kitchen is clean, no Jer, I am just joking. But we will talk after we eat.

The church members started coming in and filling up the seats. This was second Sunday, but the church was starting to fill up quickly. I look for Beth, Bob, John, Jane and Susan. I see Beth, Okay, I will be there in a minute. Hi, Beth, Hi Jerry, where are the people you invited, they are just entering the sanctuary.

What are you doing? I am going to invite them to sit with us. Is that a problem Beth, no Jer, it's not a problem, I just wanted to sit with you, by myself and was not planning to share you with anyone today. Oh, go get your friends, I'll get the seat, thanks Beth.

Hey guys we have some seat up here for you. Oh, no, man I am not going in this church and have them tell me that I am in sin. Look man! You told Jerry that you would be here and we are here so let's go in and here the word.

So, show us where you want us to sit.

Mom I am not going to church today: Bob, did I hear you correctly. Bob said no dad; I am on my way to get dress. I know that my father had a little bit to drink last night and I didn't want my father to start hitting on my mother, so I told him that I will get dress for church. Why is it that I need to go but if I don't he would use me like a punching bag along with my mother. I was moving as fast as I could to get down stairs before dad call my name again. Now; we got that phone call from Susan's parents, and you better, be praying for some answers, why you left Susan at the theater, Friday night.

Yes, dad we can talk went we get home from church. What do I have to look forward to, when I get home? My father is going to bounce me off the wall, or just knock me out. Maybe, I should have though about all of this before now: Bob let's go, don't have me keep calling you!

Okay, I am on my way down now and everyone got in the car. Bob why are you looking like your lose, nothing wrong with me, just leave me along! Hey, Bob, that is no way to speak to your sister, so you apology right now! I am sorry Donna, and don't have me stop this car. Donna I am real sorry for using that tone of voice. I will accept your apology Bob.

I know my father was upset with me and it was quiet the rest of the way to church only dad and mother said a few words as my father continued driving. As we pulled into the parking lot of the church, I saw Susan, her sister and her mother getting out of their car. Dad pulled up next to Susan mother car, and said, good morning; they exchange their greeting.

I looked at Susan and said hi. Hi Bob, all right Susan, can we talk after service? We need too. I am sorry Susan, I know you are Bob.

I wanted to say more to Susan as we walked with some distance between us, as we enter the church. The music was playing and the song was "What a fellowship". We all sat together, somehow Susan and I, where on the end seat. We kept grazing at each other and our parents were grazing at us. The choir song another selection "Amazing Grace".

I had plenty to think about, how I had to explain my action to my father and mother; and talk to Susan, and her mother as well. How stupid, I was, I knew better, but I just wanted to be mister bad boy. All the Sunday school, bible classes, sermons, religion classes, and I still; did not apply, anything. I never allowed myself to repent, or to be sorrowful, for any of my action, before now. I should have applied my faith, and believe in God; before I acted to the statement that Susan made.

What do I remember about Jesus? That he is love. Why didn't I use that with Susan a few nights ago? Beth there goes Bob and Susan and their parents entering the sanctuary. For some reason Bob face is looking a little difference today.

Good morning everyone someone is in trouble today, hey, how did the pastor know that, did my parents call him. You know that we need to pray for all things and for any situation, so let us pray before the message.

"Father as we, your children have been blessed to be in the land of the living. Oh God you have touched us this morning, you woke us up, having water to bath and to drink, clothes to put on, a roof over our head; children and everyone in our home is in their right mind with the blood running warn in their vain.

Oh Lord blessed every church that have claim Jesus as their Lord and Savior, bless those that are in the hospital, the convalescence home and those that are at home sick. Lord you know everything about everybody, just keep him or her, Lord God all mighty, in your Loving Son Jesus Name and the church said. Amen and Amen".

Sermon #1 Matt 5:43-45 The Theme is "Love" You have heard that it hath been said, Thou shalt love thy neighbour, and hate thine enemy. But I say unto you, love your enemies, bless them that curse you, do good to them that hate you, and pray for them which despitefully use you, and persecute you. That you may be the children of your Father, which is in heaven: for he maketh his sun to rise on the evil and on the good, and send rain on the just and on the unjust".

There are many other things that must, be consider in life. We all think that a relationship with others is not Importance, because he or she is not part of the same race.

But, in ones travels in life many path are cross to have some type of relationship.

We should always wonder what the purpose was for such a relationship, because some are short and other long. God use others to help us understand many of the things that make up the universe and the power that God posses all the time. There is a bond between you and that person, because it is like that person is your angle to give you direction from haven, to put you on the right path to straight street. God will use you anyway he choose too, for His glory.

Many people felt that sin should not be on any thing that they believe to be right. They will feel that sin should only be on things that they felt was wrong. That a sin was only on things that I believe to be a sin or I have not heard of it. We fail to realize, who God is and what part is played, with us to do, God's will.

Ah, The rights of the people, out weight ones personal agenda, on the style of their home, car, clothes, occupation, sexual orientation and the neighborhood you live in. Jesus, said, that we should love our neighbor, as you love yourself. This is about loving people all over the world, not just the ones that live next door, at work, in your church or community.

We, fail God's, understanding, for the kind of love he would like for us to have for each other. It does not matter who you are God loves you. St. Paul, said, we need to love one to the other. Jesus told the Jews, that I have come to return you back to your first love, God. God loves us even if we have sin, God love us.

Prostitutes, God loves them, those that lie God love them, those that commit adultery God love them, alcoholic God love them, the women and men leaving the natural use of their bodies and laying with the same sex God love them. Fornication, wickedness, covetousness, maliciousness; full of envy, murder, debate, deceit, malignity; whispers God love them.

God love them, however, God wants everyone that he loves to repent for their act of sin. And when you repent (Being godly sorry) that is when you begin to build your relationship with God. You must pick up your bible and study His Word; pray and meditate on this Word, and through your faith and devotion, fasting, praying: He will strengthen you to do His will.

You will become strong to fright off the darts (sin) of Satan through the power of God. Without the power of God, you will be unable to fight off sin, unless your faith is in God. We must understand that all of our sin, that is in us. All around us every wakening hour, and through Jesus Christ, is the only way that we can stand, not ourselves, but the God that we serve in us, I know that I am right about that saint. Amen church.

We may not be doing the same sin, but we need to come to God, for the things that we know is not of God. And stop telling; ourselves that this is what God wants me to do. Is what you are doing is it of God? God wants you to live holy, be clean and enjoy life, serving Him on this earth.

But, you see everybody, is welcome, at, Welcome Everybody Baptist Church. Amen. We must be ready with open arms to reach anyone that wishes to become a member of this church. As the pastor continued, with his sermon he took us to the cross.

I don't believe that most people are saying that they are better than someone else, it's just, that by some way or another things have worked out good for them. That's how God works, and they have better get ready went the tide turn. They never lost a job, spouse, children or love ones, no money problems, therefore; no bad credit. This is good for this person or people that have been blessed to not have problems or difficulties in their life.

But let me tell you that "Jesus was born to Mary His earthly mother. Jesus walked on this earth for thirty-three years and was preaching and healing people for three years and He was nailed to that cross for your sins and mind: He had blood and water, that ran down His side.

And the Roman solider tried to gave Him some vinegar in a sprang; attached to the spear to drink, but Jesus refuse to drink it. And—— a-bout the—nine—hour Jesus—- cried out with—in a-loud—voice, saying E'li,E'li, la'ma sa-bach'tha-ni? And——that is to say, My God, my God, why——hast—thou—forsaken——me?

Then he hung his head and dried. He was placed in another man tomb and stay there all day Friday and all night, all day Saturday, and than early——,early—! On this third day Sunday morning Jesus go up and said, all power that's been given unto me as he stood on the land and the sea." Amen—Amen-Amen.

Jerry, some members are shouting: that's because of the joy they know in Jesus, and they knew that Jesus had saw them through many of hard times, and tribulation. I am telling you right now, if you don't know Him; do you want to know Him: The doors of the church are open (meaning come and be a member of this church).

You can join by letter, water baptism, or Christian experience; is there one that will take the right hand of fellowship. Deacon William, and Deacon Jones; are here to bring you into the church. Look Beth, some men and women are jointing the church. You see Jerry there goes a few of your friends that you invited are jointing the church. Jerry we really never know, what God is up to, but God tests us everyday to see; what we are really about. Him, or ourselves. Beth let's wait for my friends. I would like to talk with them.

I think the pastor sermon really hit home, maybe we need to take sometime to talk about, what is really going on between the two of us. Jane, are those tears from the sermon? I know that it touch a number of people. But I feel like your putting pressure on me, to due all the things that you want, without understanding any of the things that I want or what is best for this relationship?

John, I agree, we need to talk about the things that are causing a problem for us. Can I start first, because I am a lady, okay, Jane go ahead; but don't you think that we need to get out of this traffic while your talking. I am sure you would like to have my attention, your right John. But I want to start now, as you know I have quiet a bit to talk about.

O-boy, Well, let me see; let me start at the beginning. Mary do you still like her; I am support to answer that Jane. I was not a where; that this was going to be a questions and answer session. And it's not John, okay. I feel that you still like Mary; and I had a hard time with that, so if you're saying that you love me, Why do I feel that it's Mary you really want to be with?

I love you John and I hurt in the pit of my stomach, for how I feel about you, and you told me, that you love me; but you just don't appear to be jumping for joy like I am. You ask me to married you. I said yes, and at that moment I felt that you; were happy just as I am. We started; well, I started making plans for the wedding, and you're not helping me. We were support to go to the jewelry, to shop for my ring.

You never said, how many people you wanted at the wedding, or where it's going to be held, our church or some other place, and; what about where we are going too live? But, I want you to be happy too, we are getting married not just me or is that the way you have looked at all of this, about what I have said. Wait! Don't stop me now! I want to make sure that our wedding is nice, just like every young lady wants a nice wedding.

Yes, I am shock, but can you blame me, I am happy, excited, that I am getting married, and it's to you John. I want this to be the best thing for you, in every way, especially my love, for you. Look Jane let me quickly pull this car over, so that we can get something straight.

Wait one minute Jane. Will you take my hand as we walk to this other area so that we can sit down and talk! Wait just one minute John, you just pulled the car over and got out of the car and now you want me to listen to what you have to say. Well John could you at less let me finish with what I was talking about. Jane this a nice day and yes your right I should have let you finish before I ask you out of the car and walked you over to the park bench. Jane, will you have a seat please? Now! I'll talk, remember I asked you to married me. I didn't ask Mary.

There are many things that I like about you. Your directness, your kindness, your caring, your honest, your patient, and how you like me, and how you say, you're in love with me. And, there is something that you must understand: That there is nothing going on, between Mary and I. I am in love with you; I like you, that is, the reason why I asked you to married me, I love you? What makes you afraid? Getting married; or are you thanking about divorce already.

Now! About all the things that you said, we needed to do, or make decision on, can we take some time to put them on paper, so that we can address them? I am not trying to down play; your excitement I am just praying to God, that I would be able to love you more and more as the years come and go. John, I think we need to talk about; sex, children, money, a home, honeymoon, in-laws, the wedding party, pastor and anything else, right now.

I just want to kiss you John. I don't know about any other young lady, you've been with; but I wanted to please you, and not have you run off. I haven't done those thing, sex. Dose that make a difference John, how do you feel about me after me telling you that? I love you Jane.

John, maybe four children; four children; I guess we will be busy with family. John, I just want our marriage to be blessed by God; and whatever the number of children are it will be all right with me, John. I guess we can work on what we are bless with, until we get it right.

Okay, what do you think the cost of the wedding is going to be? Well, we must make some phone calls for the grown, men tuxedo, rental of the hall, cost for the pastor, the catering, and limousine service. How much can we afford to spend? Less get a cost from the items that we must use for the wedding, then we are going to know the exact cost. Let's check the flowers also.

Family and friends; how many people did you have in mind to invite? What about 250 people total at the hall? You know that aunts; uncle's, grandparents are going to want to come. Let's find a nice place for our honeymoon; but not to expensive, because of the cost of the wedding. Well, I have no ideal, if we are going to be able to purchase a home, in our first year John.

That is not what I asked, no. Where are we going to live; at home is nice, an apartment, where?

I know it's take money for a home, may be if we work and save our money we can purchase it later. I want to be able, to love you John, without all the additional pressure of a mortgage payment and other things for the house.

John, I need to tell you. I spoke to my doctor to fine out about birth control pills. What do you think? Well how long are you planning to remain on them? I was thinking for the first year or maybe two years. Two years; Yes, so we can have more time to really work on each other, and learn more about our faith as we pray to God and study His Word.

Okay, Jane have you told anyone that we are planning to get married? No, not yet John, that's good, because I need to speak to your father. He may not want me to married you. You see Jane, I design this computer chip. I call it the X100 and this Company BMIIV: who has contracted me, and I will be at the new University here at home and they will pay me royalties for this chip design.

That is great John! I know you told me about a surprise that you were going to share with me; congratulation, John. So John, dose that mean, we don't have a money issue, like I though. That's right Jane! Jane, I know that you said you are going to attend college here. So we can still see each other everyday. Look John, don't you think that we need to finish college first before we get married?

Anyway, maybe we need to date other people, so down the road, we are not looking to be with, someone else, and not with, each other. I just don't. Wait! Jane, I know I don't know everything about you and nor do you know everything about me.

And, yes, we would be a young couple. Okay, Jane, let me said this. John, I do understand how you feel, because had this not been in the pit of my stomach, and saying all of that to you did not help me; with my feeling toward you, I need you to help me John.

Jane, you don't need to cry about this, we just need to talk to our parents to find out how they feel about our planning to get married.

You know John, I feel a little upset, but I know, I need to speak to my parents about this, because this is a big step in my life and I want to make sure that I am truly understanding how much work is in a marriage.

That will be good Jane, your parents will have the information about what we are planning to do and so will my parents. And this will help us make some sound decision.

Jane, you were right, no not about dating someone else, but to discuss dating other people or wanting to date other people, after we are married. Maybe we should wait until we graduated from college or wait until after we complete our first year of college before we become engage.

John, I am glad you made that clear, I just didn't know; what we were going to do? You see Jane, where working together on thing already.

Chapter 4

The Spirit of Love

Beth, we need to think about our future and how important school is for each of us. Well we need to wait until our junior year of school and if we remain together, then we can get married, then maybe one of us can transfer are credits to the other ones school.

You know that we must remain in touch with each other, but to make sure that we are focus on God and each other. Hey, I don't know Beth about all that's been said, but we talked and I know what we said, but I love you, there must be another way to resolve this distant issue. You know we just need to continue thinking and talking about it until we find the answer.

Well, we have this as our homework, that will help us to rest a little easier when we fine the answer. Oh, their Bob and Susan standing in the parking lot talking. I wonder, if Susan and Bob had an opportunity to talk about, last Friday night incident? Okay, Beth that's good, we'll just go home: why don't you call Susan later to find out how her conversion went with Bob. Beth, they see us; just wave to Bob and Susan, and keep walking to our cars.

Susan, I don't know, where to start? How about, Friday night, at the move theater, Bob? Well Susan? I was really playing around, but I guess I felt challenge, when you kept comparing me to Chad: so I just said, ya. I didn't want any more heat about the move. But Bob: Why did you just leave me, because I push you there? I felt that you had, Susan, but I should have known better and let it go, and enjoyed the movie. You know Bob we have had a discussion about how we should live. Let me see if I can find it in my bible. Okay here it is in Romans. Let me read this Bob, "Rules for Christian Living-Romans 12:9-21Let love be without dissimulation.

Abhor that which is evil; cleave to that which is good. Be kindly affection one to another with brotherly love; in honour preferring one another; Not slothful in business; fervent in spirit; serving the Lord; Rejoicing in hope; patient in tribulation; continuing instant in prayer;

Distributing to the necessity of saints; given to hospitality. Bless them, which persecute you: bless, and curse not. Rejoice with them that do rejoice, and weep with them that weep. Be of the same mind, one toward another. Mind not high things, but condscend to men of low estate. Be not wise in your own conceits.

Recompense to no man evil for evil. Provide things honest in the slight of all men. If it be possible, as much as lieth in you, live peaceably with all men. Dearly beloved; avenge not yourselves, but rather give place unto wrath: for it is written,

Vengeance is mine; I will repay, saith the Lord.

Therefore, if thin enemy hunger, feed him; if he thrist, give him drink: for in so doing thou shalt heap coals of fire on his head. Be not overcome of evil, but overcome evil with good."

"All right I guess I can take part of the blame for egging you on about that movie. But, Bob you left me there, ten miles away from home; if Jerry wasn't there, them what Bob?" "Look, Susan, please don't hate me, I do care, and I didn't want anything to happen to you.

I know your not going to forgive me, but I would love it, if you did. I am going to ask you any how, if you will forgive me anyway." "Susan, said, please Bob get off the ground," "forgive me for being so stupid in our conversation, and leaving you at the theater. I will never leave you anywhere again, I promise. But can we keep talking to each other, Susan?"

"Yes Bob, and please don't, ever do this to me again, I still love you Robert. Now put me down Bob, I don't think your out of the woods yet. You still need to show me that all of this conversation is for real and just not talk. You don't need to kiss me at less not in the church parking lot." "I was just going to kiss you on the chick." "Okay, I though that you were going to do one of those throw down kisses. You know, but not hear Bob when things are really better between us. We need to talk to our parents, about our conversation;" "yes your right Susan." "I will have my parents come by your house on our way home. Dad, Susan and I have been talking and I said, that we can stop by their home on our way home." "Well Bob this is just a statement; about what you did to Susan, on Friday night. Yes, dad.

Hi, Mr. Jones, Bob tell me that we are coming over to discuss the incident, that happen on Friday night." "Okay, That should be fine with us the sooner the better."

We all arrived at Susan's parent's home, around the same time. Dad parked, and we enter through the front of the house. Susan and her mother service tea to everyone, and Donna went to the bonus room to watch television, with Susan's, sister, Kathy.

"Well Mr. And Mrs. Jones, I have apologize to Susan for what I did on Friday night at the theater; and I hope that you will find it in your heart to forgive me also. Susan and I did talk after church today and that is the reason we are here now? Sir if there is anything that I can do to show my sincerity, let me know." "Bob's father said, I got something for you, okay."

"Well, Mr. and Mrs. Jones, thank you for everything." "And we will talk, when we get home Bob." "Bob please call me okay. Okay Susan."

"Well we better be on our way home. Bob, I am glad you decided to talk to Mr. & Mrs. Jones, before I had a chance to say something to you. I am not saying that you're going to get the car back right away, but I will think about how much time you are going to receive, before you get the car back. It's going to be some time, but it's not going to be two months." "Dad, I know you're going to be fair, you and mother. I need you and mother to help me, get to work on my part-time job, okay."

"Bob, one of us will take you to work when it is needed. Son let's go and eat your mother cooking, they are waiting for us."

Beth, don't forget bible class, Monday night at 7:00 P.M. I will call John and Bob to see if they are going to be there." "Okay, Jerry, I will call Jane and Susan to find out if they are planing to attend? I'll see you tomorrow Jerry."

Hey, John, are you planing to attend bible class, tomorrow night? Yes Jerry. Have you spoken to Bob yet? No I haven, have you. No.

Jerry I'll call Bob, to find out if he is going to attend bible class, okay. Yes John, I'll talk to you later; see yea. Hey Bob, this is John, what's up Bob: Nothing John. Are you going to bible class tomorrow night: oh, ha, yea, man I need to go. Hey man, I made a mistake, and believe you me; I am paying for all of it, right about now.

From my dad and mother: to Susan parents and Susan. Guess what John? What: Susan forgave me, oh she did Bob, that's great man. So dose that mean you guys are still together, will John, I am not saying that we are not; but I must call Susan tonight and talk.

I hope the two of you can really work out everything, I am going to tell Jane. She will be very happy to hear that you and Susan are trying to make-up. Hey man: I am going to catch you later, okay John, see you tomorrow night, be cool.

You know that's right, dating is hard, when you have the wrong spirit; in you. About how you should treat another person. It's not about you trying to have your way, or trying to control someone, when it should be about love, kindness, respect and God: are some of the key component to form a relationship.

Many of the young people are thinking that it should be about sex and they will think about love, at another time in their life. After Susan read the scripture I felt that I understood more about; what we men need to understand; love is not sex, and sex is not love. They are different, and it is very important that we understand, what and how those interactions are applied in the marital relationship. When love is at the highest level as we understand God's Word: having intercourse is the gift that God gave to husbands and wife. If you are married, making love becomes, very high if you have God in the center of your marriage or very low when one person does not apply the Word's of God, in the relationship. I see how my father and mother act when my father is drinking and many problems are discussed and I wonder if my father is allowing God's Word into his spirit. Like Susan, this is another scripture that was shared with our class, on our spirit. Let me read this again. St. Matthew 5:16 "Let your light so shine before men, that they may see your good works, and glorify your Father which is in heaven."

Oh, man it's Monday, morning and we got to get ready for school. I hear my brothers and sister moving around I guess my father and mother are all ready down stairs to go to work. I had to make sure that we were out of the house by 7:00 A.M. Look children, give me and your father a hug and we will see after we get home from work.

There are many times that I am thinking about, because I am the oldest child in this family and understand that all families are not a like. I just envision the families that are split, because of drugs, father have left, mother have left, use of alcohol, adoption, and homosexual activity. We have a lot of people in this world that are hurting and that is a major affect on the families.

There are many tough decision that are made each day, and every day, by parents or children if there are no parents, about what they will do on this day, and every day after this day.

Little do we know or understand how importance it is to have parents. They make it their business to stray on top of us; help us do well in school, and at home, in the community, at church and any were else we would need to be, to do the right things. That is, why I know that the bible tell us as a child; we should make sure that we listen to our parents. Just like these scripture instruct us on how to act and what we should be doing.

Proverbs 22:6 "Train up a child in the way he should go: and when he is old, he will not depart from it."

Ephesians 6:1-4 "Children, obey your parents in the Lord: for this is right. Honor your father and mother;

which is the first commandment with promise; That it may be well with thee, and thou mayest live long on the earth. And, ye fathers, provoke not your children to wrath: but bring them up in the nurture and admonition of the Lord."

Colossians 3:20-21 "Children, obey your parents in all things: for this is well pleasing unto the Lord. Fathers, provoke not your children to anger, lest they be discouraged."

Chapter 5

Why Did I Get Married? For Love And For Making Love.

Hey, guys how was school today; let us eat super before we go to bible class. Make sure that your homework is completed before we leave for church. Oh, Paul it's almost time for us to leave for bible class, will you let the children know? Once we arrived at church we all went to our assigned class. Okay, Jerry make sure that everyone is out hear once class has ended. See you then.

Hi, everyone have the pastor made it yet. Oh, yes there's the Pastor now. Pastor Johnson is teaching the adult bible class; the class ended with marriage. Okay everyone do you remember the question. "Why did I get married?" and "What is marriage?" Reverend William will take the junior class Deacon Barns will have the youth. The adults class will remain hear. Good evening, everyone: let us pray. "Father, thank you for touching us this morning allowing us to travel to work, and then come out this night for more bible training: bless them that are in the hospital; the ones at home, and the ones in the convenience home: blessing everyone in Jesus name. Amen! Amen! Amen!

All right, we are going to continue, with our discussion from last week on marriage: Sister Walker. What was your comment on last week? Well Pastor since you re-mined me that I said something. Oh, yes, I was asking about the types of problems that married couples have; like money, communication, and making love. I didn't hear that last one Sister Walker,

I said, making love! Okay sister; okay Sister Walker. What is your point Sister Walker?

Why, do men think that it's the women that don't want to make love? May be they just don't want to make love, with him any longer. Oh, Wait! Wait! Sister Walker, we are talking about married couples, and not about singles people. Because for singles, that will be fornication, which is a sin, if they were making love. Intercourse is just for men and women that are married to each other.

Now, let me go to the bible. St. Paul explains that there was a misunderstanding about marriage, also people thinking that it was sinful to live unmarried. St. Paul said, that it was good that one will abstain from marriage; because of the Christian church they would keep themselves single, and not have sex, in order that they do not sin.

He informs them that marriage, and the comforts and satisfactions of that state, are prescribed by Divine wisdom. Nor ought married persons to imagine it is right for them to live long a part.

First, this is, what it say in Genesis 29:20-21 "And Jacob served seven years for Rachel; and they seemed unto him but a few days, for the love he had to her.

And Jacob said unto Laban, Give me my wife, for my days are fulfilled, that I may go in unto her."

I Corinthians 7:1-11 "Now concerning the things whereof ye wrote unto me: It is good for a man not to touch a women. Nevertheless, to avoid fornication, let every man have his own wife, and let every women have her own husband. Let the husband render unto the wife due benevolence: and likewise also the wife unto the husband.

The wife has not power of her own body, but the husband: and likewise also the husband hath not power of his own body, but the wife. Defraud you not one the other, except it be with consent for a time, that ye may give yourselves to fashing and prayer; and come together again, that Satan tempt you not for your incontinency.

But I speak this by permission, and not of commandment. For I would that all men were even as I myself. But every man hath his proper gift of God, one after this manner, and if they and another after that. I say therefore to the unmarried and widows, It is good for them if they abide even as I. But if they cannot contain, let them marry: for it is better to marry than to burn.

And unto the married I command, yet not I, but the Lord, let not the wife depart from her husband: But and if she depart, let her remain unmarried, or be reconciled to her husband: and let not the husband put away his wife."

Proverbs 18:20-24 "A man's belly shall be satisfied with the fruit of his mouth; and with the increase of his lips shall he be filled.

Death and life are in the power of the tongue: and they that love it shall eat the fruit thereof. Whoever so fine a wife findeth a good thing, and obtaineth favour of the Lord. The poor use intreaties; but the rich answer roughly. A men that hath friends must shew himself friendly: and there is a friend that sticketh closer than a brother."

"Some marriage rules for Christian Living-Colossians 3:16-21 Let the word of God dwell in you richly in all wisdom; teaching and admonishing one another in Psalms and hymns and spiritual songs, singing with grace in your hearts to the Lord. And whatsoever ye do inword or deed, do all in the name of the Lord Jesus, giving thanks to God and the Father by him.

Wives, submit yourselves unto your own husbands, as it is fit in the Lord. Husbands, love your wives, and be not bitter against them. Children, obey your parents in all things: for this is well pleasing unto the Lord. Fathers, provoke not your children to anger, lest they be discouraged."

Well Pastor what about the power and control over one another body, okay, Deacon Jones, a very good question, I am sure, the sisters will have a great deal to say about this question and because: I just read the answer to this question.

Now before, the sisters, start a discussion let me eject this process, about our singles and how children will have a different social challenge. The single female will be challenge; having the full responsibility of rearing her children or child without their father. It is more difficult, when your singleness, came out of a divorce.

Because, it would be hard for the children to understand the separation; when the parents have talked about: love, forgiveness, being kind, and teaching them about the bible: Now you must explain, sharing custody, of the children, with the father. Young girl may grow up; with trust issues not sure: if they are truly in love with this man. Because, the type, of bond that she has is with a female (mother), and she has learn how to only trust a female. Because, she has heard and saw, how her mother have or was treated by a man.

Male children, in a single female household, will lean on the women to support him, as they become men, because, their mother have supported him. She would not spend a great deal of time, trying to push him out of the house; to get a job, so he would support himself, and a family.

The mother will feel, whatever money he makes, he should think of her first, and not some other female or get married and leave her along. After all she (the mother) had taken care of him all his live.

When both parents rear the children the daughter is looking for a man that will treat her in the same manner that her father has, with respect, understanding, caring, being respectful in conversation, truthful and honest: and will bring happiness to the relationship.

Men are looking for the same things in a wife; when he has both parents. That he looked at his parents, in how they respond to each other on all issues; that he has heard discuss.

When there is a different from husband or wife it makes husband or wife wonder, what went wrong and what is the problem? With him or her: Because, as the man; he is employing, what he saw from his father how to address issues with his wife: and the wife is employing, some of the method that she saw her mother used on her father.

So, why isn't it not working to resolve the issue to their problems? Pastor can you help. These methods only work when both husband and wife have a true relationship with God. By the grace of God, you must be willing to forgive or ask for, forgiveness, because of their action or attitude.

Unless husband and wife are in Christ Jesus, it will be an unreasonable challenge, and the result may end up in divorce. I didn't say people going or coming to the church building are in a relationship, with Christ Jesus. I said, you must have a relationship, with Christ Jesus, so that you both know that you must go into prayer about; whatever the problem is; and than go to the other person, husband or wife and ask for, forgiveness.

And female children have a challenge or dislike of men attitude because of how their mother had been treated, so they may be defending their position, about what men say; and how men respond to them. So, men may have had a difficult time after they get married; to these female in a single parent household, and the man not knowing; why his wife act and respond the way she dose to him.

Deacon Jones, you have something to add. Yes, it dose may it very challenging. I understand how sweet and loving I need to be to my wife, but sometimes; my wife just say things, just to bring about an argument. So, the bible tells us to be like Christ: and we are some times. But it becomes very hard to deal with this behavior. Even when the scripture say; your wife body is yours, and your body is your wife.

Okay, one at a time Sister Jones, you mean to tell me, my husband can have me any time he wants. I don't think so Pastor, this is my body, and if I don't feel like doing anything, then I won't. Okay Sister Jones, why would you, not feel like being intimacy or doing anything, with the person that you said, you're in love with?

Because, he may had said, something I didn't like, or if some thing upset me at work or I am just not in the mood. Where is our forgiveness, and compassion for someone we say where in love with? Now, this is a very good argument; as to why, Sister Jones said, she is not going to be intimate and making love, with her husband. Well Pastor, dose that gives the man the right, to get satisfaction from some other women.

Let me have the wives answer that question, because this is their body. No Pastor, Sister Grace said, it is not right for my husband to get his needs met from another women. Because, I must find some way to be understanding to his needs as his wife; and not bring bitterness home from work that would cause me to reject my husband because of junk. Now he made get rejected because I am not well, but because I am in Christ Jesus: I will always make it my responsibility to take care of his needs, because my husband always take care of my needs.

Yes, Deacon Heck, you see what is going on is not love and it not about making love. If you are in love with someone, and there is a problem; you both should think about praying to correct your attitude: so you do not give negative feelings to your spouse. As Sister Grace stated if she is sick; you should agree that there would not be any intimacy, and no love making: but the wife should not tell her husband not to touch her.

Her, body belong to him and his to her. If this is about love, because no man should fill, that his wife do not care enough for him that she is saying; No. A tally of intimacy and love making is not healthy for a godly relationship; because who really cares, unless they have a negative feeling if the number of times is too high.

As a married couple, that is one of the things, both of you should count on, that you are going to make love anytime, you want with just the person you are in love with. Anytime any way, he is yours and you are his.

Before, we get into the scripture; let me share this information, with you to help the men understand. That there may be some difficulties for women; which is out of their control, and that can impact the marriage, if they are not sure: why it happen or even how to stop it.

Well Ladies, I am here to tell you that you can not control it at all. What you need to hope and prayer for is that the man you have married is truly a man of God, because your going to need him to be patience, with you as you are going through this process of life.

Menopause; would affect every female in their life, it is a major process for women and without understanding, it will end many marriage. The process of menopause will make the wife appear to be a Dr. Jekyll and Mr. Hyde. The mood swing that will keep men off balance, in the relationship, and it may have then look for comfort from another women that in many cases she would be younger.

So, women may have had and operation; you need to inform your husband that this may impact your mood; due to your estrogen level is affected and your estrogen sexual hormone would have declined.

Because, estrogen is essential for reproduction, it also, would affect other organs in the body. Cells in the Vagina, bladder, breasts, skin, bones, arteries, heart, liver and brain: all contain estrogen receptors, and requires this hormone to stimulate these receptors for normal cell function. Because of the lower level of estrogen this would lower your desire for lovemaking.

There are difference risks for men, which is their prostate. If men have prostate infections it may have occurred because, of there sexually history with diseases, and alcohol use. Which, can cause congestion of the prostate gland, and it can be a breeding ground for various bacteria.

It is so important that we understand that God; has designed a function or process of prayer that will help the man or women understand; why they got married in the first place, love we hope. This stop point, were your love and respect, if you are in God, will carry your marriage through this rough patch in your relationship. Because of your faith and your wife faith; God will see your marriage through, where your intimacy will be restored, as long as you are leaning on Christ Jesus.

Let's read the other scripture and than discuss them.

If we look at Deuteronomy 24:5 "When a men have taken a new wife, he shall not go out to war, neither shall he be charged with any business: but he shall be free at home one year, and shall cheer up his wife which he has taken."

Also, Proverbs 5:16-20 "Let your fountains be dispersed abroad, and rivers of water in the streets. Let them be only your own, and not strangers' with you. Let their fountain be blessed: and rejoice with the wife of your youth. Let her be as the loving hind and pleasant roe; let her breasts satisfy you at all times; and be thou ravished always with her love. And why wilt thou, my son, be ravished with a strange woman, and embrace the bosom of a stranger?"

Colossians 3:18-19 "Wives, submit yourselves unto your own husbands, as it is fit in the Lord. Husbands, love your wives, and be not bitter against them." Hebrew 13:4 "Marriage is honorable in all, and the bed undefiled: but whore mongers and adulterers God will judge."

Pastor, yes Deacon Walker, I just wanted to say that women fantasy of marriage is up beat until realty comes in, then the husband is the worse person on earth. When the wife find that everything that she wants to buy, create, or build is not always going to happen just like she wants it, it becomes a problem.

This is a problem, because of the emotion of females, it effects every spiritual, and human feeling of her body.

Yes, it dose. It is the estrogen level Deacon Walker, yes Pastor. We all have disappointments, but the type of dependence, she has to that disappointment; the man will fine himself in the wind or in the doghouse.

She will not tell him, why she is feeling the way that she feels, because she will tell you, that you need to finger that out and give her an apology: for what you don't know; what you have done? But, if the husband acted like the wife, she would tell him to grow up and act like a man.

It is too, bad that the husbands cannot tell their wife to grow up and act like a lady; because she is acting like a lady. The true statement is, wives in Christ, has a since of responsibility and will think about what her husband stated to her, and think less about what is good for her and more about; what is good for the family.

This statement is what the wives always want the husbands to think like at all times. I just want to say to the husbands we must always keep in mind that the marriage is not just for the women. To keep her from looking like a prostitute, but also for the man, to keep him from acting like a rabbit, as well; jumping from bed to bed.

But, with God, He will put stability in the life of the man and woman, to serve Him and be honorable to God in all things; to appreciate, love, joy, likeness, have kindness toward each other, husband and wife. Remember God, gave a place to the wife after she was tempted by the Serpent, to have children and the labor of it, to remind her, of her disobedience to God and to her husband. Now, let us look at this scripture.

I Timothy 2:9-15 "In like manner also, that the women adorn themselves in modest apparel, with shame face and sobriety; not with broided hair, or gold, or pearls, or costly array; But (which become women professing godliness) with good works. Let the women learn in silence with all subjection. But I suffer not a woman to teach, nor to usurp authority over the man, but to be in silence.

For Adam was first formed; then Eve. And Adam was not deceived, but the woman being deceived was in the transgression. Notwithstanding she shall be saved in childbearing, if they continue in faith and charity and holiness with sobriety."

"I Corinthians 11:1-19 Be you followers of me, even as I also am of Christ. Now I praise you, brethren, that ye remember me in all things, and keep the ordinances, as I delivered them to you. But I would have you to know, that the head of every man is Christ; and the head of the woman is the man; and the head of Christ is God.

Every man praying or prophesying, having his head covered, dishonor his head. But every woman that prayeth or prophesieh with her head uncovered dishonoureth her head; for that is even all one as if she were shaven. For if the woman be not covered, let her also be shorn: but if it be a shame for a woman to be shorn or shaven, let her be covered.

For a man indeed ought not to cover his head, forasmuch; as he is the image and glory of God: but the woman is the glory of the man. For the man is not of the woman; but the woman of the man. Neither was the man created for the woman; but the woman for the man. For this cause ought the woman to have power on her head because of the angels. Never the less neither is the man without the woman, neither the woman is without the man, in the Lord.

For as the woman is of the man, even so is the man also by the woman; but all things of God. Judge in yourselves: is it right for a woman pray unto God uncovered? Do not even nature itself teach you, that, if a man have long hair, it is a shame unto him?

But if a woman have long hair, it is a glory to her:

for her hair is given her for a covering. But if any man seem to be contentious, we have no such custom, neither the churches of God. Now in this that I declare unto you I praise you not, that ye come together not for the better, but for the worse.

For first of all, when ye come together in the church, I hear that there be divisions among you; and I partly believe it. For there must be also heresies among you, that they which are approved may be made manifest among you."

Man is not in his rightful place in God; therefore, he is not right in the home and with his wife and children. The wife is not in her rightful place in God, therefore, she is not right in the home, and with her husband and children.

We need to spend less times pointing out ones another negatives, and more time praying to God, and studying God's Word to get right before Him; to get God Word Right; to have the spirit of God in us.

Wives because the bible state, husband love your wives, as Christ love the church. That does not mean, that the wife, do not need to make some sacrifices, for her husband and for the children (it's not all about you).

Husbands, you have a real hard job focusing on God, to keep your wife happy and to have Gods, understanding, to remain true to your wife.

By, us being real in Christ we can be real at the time that we married, fully understanding, sex, money, communication, respect, children, purchases, and education are a part of the marriage.

If we love spending money; why have we stopped; the love making. If we love, making love, why have we stopped communicating? If we love communicating how come we have no respect? If we love our children, why have we not provided for their care and education?

Marriage is the only earthly journey; were you have a great deal of your trials and tribulations, from your husband or wife or children and you must be as Christ to forgive them, and give them unconditionally love.

Now with these few scriptures lets open the discussion up Sister Walker, I know you have had your hands up, to jump in. Okay Sister Walker, okay Pastor, thank you I had to hold on, I had to keep re-minding myself about what I was going to say.

Now; all of this about your husband, having control over your body. I know it's the right thing to do: but we are just being women and figure that we can control this action. Because this is our body, and hope that my husband, would not go to another women: because of my action.

Ya, okay, Pastor, so, okay my body, is my husband and he should taken care of it, that's right Pastor; yes, Sister Walker. So, I am to let him, if nothing is wrong with me to be intimate and making love any time, all the time, okay, that's good. Now, Sister Walker, the most important thing to keep in mind is being like Christ, and being in love with your spouse.

Okay now Pastor, obey, I am support to obey my husband, yes? When all the time? When is he support to obey me; because the bible did not said husband obey your wife. Okay, obey, if there are things to be done and the husband needs to make a decision, the wife needs to understand and support the husband decision.

Let's review something, okay, one minute Pastor, yes, Deacon Heck, women want to be married, because of their nature, they want the freedom to do what they want including having an affair, without the penalty that is placed on men.

Well Pastor this is what they say. My husband should feel honor, privilege, and happy, that he has me. What I have on the side is just a fling; but I love my husband.

Wait, don't you think that he is having a fling, just like you are having. No! He would fall in love with that lady and leave me for her. I can control my feeling with this other man. Any, how this is my body and I determine who I want to ride this ride. Men just ride anything. No! Men choose who they want to be with more than any women can imagine.

She is looking, for that understanding, from others about what she have done. And, not to be, judged the way men are judge, without compassion.

Well, Deacon Heck, I understand what you just said, like Jezebel, she felt nothing would happen to her, until she was broad down like the men.

Until, the prophet Eljah, told her what was going to happen, she did not believe that, up until her death. Okay, Pastor, I feel that women have had a list to be accomplish; and once they have completed their list, they sit down.

Will, Deacon, No one can sit down, unless they do not understand God's Word and will. Just like at work, if you don't perform, you will be out of a job. We all must perform our duties, if we like it or not, or want too, or not.

Sister Grace, I think men are held to a higher standard, then women. No, sister, God has a standard and His judgment are by His standards and if women feel that, because they are a woman, that God is going to judge her less, they better stop wasting their time coming to church.

Because, men and women must go far beyond, their understanding of the bible, and must blend the bible experience, with their faith walk and Jesus Christ. The husband and wife must have a pervasive role with Christ: to ensure the homiletics of their relationship, with God.

If we choose to believe it, or not, there is a covenant for marriage with God. So they will have a responsible relationship of obedience to God, and to each other. And live the embodiment of freedom for their marriage liberation.

Chapter 6

Who Changed the Truth of God?

Because, Satan home is where they will be, if you have not made a commitment to God. It's not based on male or female, but on your faith, and believe in Him, and on Him. Well Pastor, Bro. Earnest, the women by nature is some what spiritual in nature, but not spiritual in act or commitment.

She must be re-minded of her commitment by, and only with the scripture doctrine; how she will be held accountable, for her life in Christ. Yes, your right brother, because men are going to answer to God, for how he worked, and if he is married; how he has treated his wife and children.

Ah, Ah, Pastor Johnson, yes, Sister Walker, the man must know and understand that he must be in Christ; at all times to receive his just blessing from God. And the women must be in Christ; at all times to receive her just blessing from God.

The man must understand that he can not control his wife. At anytime, because of her nature she will leave him, and desert him simultaneously, because of her nature. As women; we all struggle with that: who we really are, and whether our lifes reflect our true selves. And we strive to be authentic in all aspects of life, in what I am working on, or building. Look I know what it tells us in Genesis 3:4-5 it's like this saint: I feel that we aren't authentic, because of the discourse that draw Eve into a parley with the serpent. And he aimed at her sense of obligation of God command. The subjection from Satan was to blemish the reputation of the Divine Law; to make it uncertain or unreasonable, to have people in sin: it is our wisdom that keeps, up a firm belief and respect for the command of God. It was Eve weakness to enter into discourse with the serpent, she knew that the serpent did not have a good design, and therefore she should have started going back to were Adam was. But Satan promises advantage and improvements by eating the fruit, to have intellectual delight and satisfaction. So he made Eve feel discontent with their present state, like it was so bad. Ambition of preferment as if they were fit to be gods. Satan had ruined himself desiring to be like the Most High, so he wanted to infect our first parents with the same desire, that he might ruin them too.

Sister Walker, are you telling me; that women have not really committed to anyone, they are just out there, for what they can get. Well, Pastor we want to control, and cut our own way, but we are pulled down, because we need security. And we are still trying to figure out how we can accomplish the things we want; but this duty of intimacy and love making create problems for us, and we do argue just, to say no.

I just did not think that it was that important, because my mind is on other things, and not being sexual is one of them, because I am married now. You see, I got married so that I would not be alone, I wanted to be married; but I did not want the true commitment on my part to be committed to the duty of being married. I wanted my husband to be committed to being married so he would not leave me for some other women. Now, women do try to be like men, and sleep around, but that gets old, so, we married.

Okay, Sister Walker, let me read this other scripture it is in Proverbs 31:1-9 "The words of king O Lem'u-el, the prophecy that his mother taught him. What, my son? And what, the son of my womb? And what, the son of my vows? Give not their strength unto women, nor thy ways to that which destroyeth kings. It is not for kings, O Lem'u-el, it is not for kings to drink wine; nor for princes strong drink;

Lest they drink, and forget the law, and pervert the judgment of any of the afflicted. Give strong drink unto him that is ready to perish, and wine unto those that be of heavy hearts. Let him drink, and forget his poverty, and remember his misery no more. Open their mouth for the dumb in the cause of all such as are appointed to destruction. Open their mouth, judge righteously, and plead the cause of the poor and needy."

Sister Walker; the important of God in ones life is that God will control the man life to be committed to his wife, even when things are not right by his wife. God control the wife nature by His Words: for those women, that are living, and have faith, and believe in God's Words.

And so this is, how he also controls the men that are living, having faith, and believe in God's Words. Brother Robber, Pastor, I look at men and women together they make the perfect sandwich; Okay, wait Brother Robber; let me read this scripture for where your going with this. Proverbs 12:13-18 "An evil man is trapped by his sinful talk, but a righteous man escapes trouble. From the fruit of his lips a man is filled with good things as surely as the work of his hands rewards him. The way of a fool seems right to him, but a wise man listens to advice. A fool shows his annoyance at once, but a prudent man overlooks an insult. A truthful witness gives honest testimony, but a false witness tells lies. Reckless words pierce like a sword, but the tongue of the wise brings healing."

You need a mind knowledge, which is the man in Christ imagine, and the spirit of the women is the church, Christ and the church; not just Christ; or just the church; but Christ, and the church.

You are right Brother Robber; the order is God, Jesus the Christ, Man, and women. Jesus the Christ glorify, God, Man glorify Jesus the Christ, Women is the man's glory and the children are the woman glory. When we do not have things in the right order; we have confusion. Let me read this Scripture for you.

Romans 1:25-31 "They exchanged the truth of God for a lie, and worshipped and served created things rather than the Creator-who is forever praised. Amen. Because of this, God gave them over to shameful lusts. Even their women exchanged natural relations for unnatural ones, In the same way the men also abandoned natural relations with women and were inflamed with lust for one another. Men committed indecent acts with other men, and received in themselves the due penalty for their perversion. Furthermore, since they did not think it worthwhile to retain the knowledge of God, he gave them over to a depraved mind, to do what ought not to be done. They have become filled with every kind of wickedness, evil, greed and depravity. They are full of envy, murder, strife, deceit and malice. They are gossips, slanderers, God-haters, insolent, arrogant and boastful; they invent ways of doing evil; they disobey their parents; they are senseless, faithless, heartless, ruthless."

Our problems have always been with us, we have become addicted to things that are not of God. When an individual have a drug problem, he or she were not in Christ. If you have an alcoholic problem you are not in Christ. If you are a gray person you are not in Christ. If your are a lesbian, you are not in Christ, and if you have a fornication problem you are not in Christ. If you sleep around you are not in Christ; you must be in the spirit of God, to ward off sin on every corner.

For what every the reason that we want anything, to be accepted by others, just to make it all right, is far reaching. But, it is God, that said, these things are a sin. So, you need to see God about your sins. If you and your wife make love every day of the week, you both are doing your duty; having power over each other body according to scripture.

I Corinthian 7:4-5 "The wife has not power of her own body, but the husband: and likewise also the Husband has not power of his own body, but the wife. Defraud you not one the other, except it be with consent for a time, that you may give yourselves to fasting and prayer; and come together again, that Satan tempt you not for your incontinence."

Now if you are single you are not to be sexual that's fornication with another person. Here are the scriptures. I Corinthians 5:9-13 "I wrote unto you in an epistle not to company with fornicator: Yet not altogether with the fornicators of the world, or with the covetous, or extortion, or with idolaters; for then must you needs go out of the world. But now I have written unto you not to keep company, if any man is called a brother be a fornicator, or covetous, or an idolater, or a rail, or a drunkard, or an extortion, with such an one on not to eat. For what have I to do to judge them also that are without? Do not you judge them that are within? But them that are, without God judge. Therefore put away from among yourselves that wicked person."

Sister Black, you have something to say, yes Pastor, there are many things that men don't know about women. The times we spend with them are for what we can get, not trying really to get to know him. Wait! Wait! Ah ah, Sister Black you have gotten the sisters upset, and the brothers want to understand: what do you really mean by that statement.

Ah, Pastor, let me help Sister Black out okay, okay, Sister Grace. We work the men to get what we want or what we want to have. It's not that men, are not a where that this is going on, it's just that most men, figure that it's not going to happen to them; because we tell them, that we are in Christ.

Okay, let me understand this you sisters are stating this, because, of what? Sister Grace, because until we come to Christ, for real, we are trying to play like men, it just that men understand things, and they can get away with it. We can, but we may need to go to another country if we wanted to be married. We would be called names (for ladies of the street), that are degrading. So, to even the playing field, we push to get married. Let me read this scripture to you, from Romans.

"Love-Romans 13:7-11 Render therefore to all their dues: tribute to whom tribute is due; custom to whom custom; fear to whom fear; honour to whom honour. Owe no man any thing, but to love one another: for he that loveth another hath fulfilled the law.

For this, Thou shalt not commit adultery, Thou shalt not kill, Thou shalt not steal, Thou shalt not bear false witness, Thou shalt not covet; and if there be any other commandment, it is briefly comprehended in this saying, namely, Thou shalt love they neighbour as thyself.

Love, work no ill to his neighbour: therefore love is the fulfilling of the law. And that, knowing the time, that now it is high time to awake out of sleep: for now is our salvation nearer than when we believed."

Okay sister Grace go ahead, because, women can not be out here like men, because, we want to be looked at, as a lady, not a prostitute. So we work on getting married, but we did not understand the amount or the type of sex drive that our husband would still have after the honeymoon.

So now we are married, and we know longer want to make love, why Deacon Grace asked. Well, because we have done it all, with our husband already, so why do we need to repeat the same thing over, and over again; each night, or once week or once month. We already know what the out come is going to be.

Okay, so Sister Grace, dose that mean that you are willing to let your marriage go to have some pace? No, Pastor, the problem real is that we can not make up our minds, on many things, and it is design by nature.

We tell ourselves, that it is not our nature, but it is, and if it's not, then we just lied and we are deep in sin or both.

Wait, a minute Sister Grace, why would you wives refuse making love one night, and than want to make love, with your husband the next night. Is it, because he have told you that he has a bonus check for a few thousands dollars or that he is going to leave you. Is that when you realized that you have not done your service to your husband.

Now, Brother Green, if your wife dose not want to make love, with you, and then change her mind the next day, because of money, or because you said that your leaving. One, she is not in love with you; two, she just love money; three by your planning to leave put her on notice that she must take care of herself; and four she is in sin, and not in Christ Jesus. If any women or men married, and it wasn't for being in love, they are in sin and they are a liar.

It's not that men say anything, because some are men of God, and I know that my husband have always been in prayer about, how I have treated him. When I refuse making love with him; I know he was upset, but he will always prayer about it, and our family: so I know that he went into prayer about me not doing my duty as a wife, to her husband.

Wait! Wait! Sister Grace, yes, Pastor, oh what's wrong Deacon Grace; I just wanted to ask Sister Grace; so what dose that mean to our marriage. Nothing, marriage is great and all women want it. It is the most important thing in any female life not children.

Marriage means that this man is willing to take me; with all my issues of being a female, and on top of that, he chose me out of so many other women: but he chose me. And I will do nothing that will hurt or harm him; and I know that I can destroy this relationship quickly: and faster than when I got in it by acting selfish; trying to control him and not truly being a wife, and lover to my husband. Pastor do you have any more scripture? Yes hear it is, Trials and Temptations- "James 1:12-18 Blessed is the man that endureth temptation: for when he is tried, he shall receive the crown of life, which the Lord hath promised to them that love him. Let no man say when he is tempted, I am tempted of God: for God cannot be tempted with evil, neither tempteth he any man: But every man is tempted, when he is drawn away of his own lust, and enticed. Then when lust hath conceived, it bringeth forth sin: and sin, when it is finished, bringeth forth death. Do not err, my beloved brethern. Every good gift and every perfect gift is from above, and cometh down from above, and cometh down from the Father of lights, with whom is no variableness, neither shadow of turning.

Of his own will begat he us with the word of truth, that we should be a kind of firstfruits of his creatures. Wherefore, my beloved brethern, let every man be swift to hear, slow to speak, slow to wrath: For the wrath of man worketh not the righteousness of God."

Hold it! Hold it! Sister Grace, let this old sister jump in, too, let me break this down from the marriage point a view. Okay Sister Walker, well I don't know where, I am going to start; I am just going to jump in right here. Love making on the honeymoon and money all that juicy sex will end shortly after the honeymoon.

Why, because I figure my job is done, because where married now. But little do ninety-five percent of the women realize that men do not slow down there desired for love making after the honeymoon. In the majority of marriages the love making for most men increases, and the wife decreases.

Because, she think, she has accomplish a goal, and she is now trying to control or find something or some way to wear her husband down so he would not want to make love every night.

You see the thing that women do not understand is that it dose not manner; how much work the man is doing at bedtime he wants to make love.

And she is trying to keep it from him trying to control his sex drive. The true of the manner is we are putting our marriage under, and giving our husband and excuse to sleep around. Well if you taken care of him at home then he has no reason to Rome.

Let me said something, okay Sister Grace. Sister Walker is right. We as women don't know and don't try to understand our husband sexual appetite. We just tell ourselves this every night, or two times a week or when he feel that he want to make love is going to stop.

We women our blessed to have found a husband that is serving God, and we say that we are following who? Because, it is not God that you are following because if you follow God, He will protect you; so that your husband is not going to hurt you with his sexual wants. We are not God, therefore, that is the reason we find it hard being married, because we do not commit to God, to obey our husbands.

Okay, let me read this scripture to you in "Proverbs 2 My son, if thou wilt receive my words, and hide my commandments with thee; So that thou incline thine ear unto wisdom, and apply thine heart to understanding; Yea, if thou criest after knowledge, and liftest up thy voice for understanding; If they seek her as silver, and searchest for her as for hid treasures; Then shall they understand the fear of the Lord, and find the knowledge of God. For the Lord giveth wisdom: out of his mouth cometh knowledge and understanding. He lay up sound wisdom for the righteous: he is a buckler to them that walk uprightly.

He keep the paths of judgment and preserve the way of his saints. Then shall they understand righteousness, and judgment, and equity; yea, every good path. When wisdom enter into thine heart, and knowledge is pleasant unto thy soul;

Discretion shall preserve thee, understanding shall keep thee: To deliver you from the way of the evil man, from the man that speaketh froward things. Who leave the paths of unrighteousness, to walk in the ways of darkness; who rejoice to do evil, and delight in the frowardness of the wicked. whose ways are crooked, and they froward in their paths: To deliver you from the strange woman, even from the stranger which flattereth with her words. Which for sake the guide of her youth, and forget the covenant of her God. For her house inclineth unto death, and her paths unto the dead. None that go unto her return again neither take hold of the paths of life.

That they may walk in the way, of good men and keep the paths of the righteous. For the upright shall dwell in the land, and the perfect shall remain in it. But the wicked shall be cut off from the earth, and the transgressors shall be rooted out of it."

You see the process of things we must be careful of not to make decision about things, because that is what we want to do. Go a head sister. There is no discussing we just stop the love making, because were trying to control him, we feel out of control, because we really do not know how to say I have a problem. However: Stop! is not the word to use? I think the problem is we as women lying to our husbands making them think they are going to make love; when they wanted it, telling them you can have all that: before the honeymoon, and after the honeymoon. To be honest, we sold our husband a lie, and we tried to back out of it once we got most of what we wanted.

Let me be honest; I love, making love, but when I want it. My husband Deacon Grace asked me after we were married for a few months. What is wrong? I told him nothing, I didn't want to tell him: that I didn't want sex as much as he did. So he said, Diane, what is it that you want, and what are you looking for.

This is what I said. I don't know: I feel cheap having sex all the time, he said, look at me. Diane is it me that make you feel cheap, or is it the act that makes you feel cheap. I said the act makes me feel cheap. He said, let me tell you this Diane; it really doesn't manner how you feel about the act: I love you. Someone else just may want the act and they may not love you the way that I do.

And because, both of us said, before we were married that we loved, and obey God's commandments: than we need to review our vows and study the scripture on marriage. We really should not be going down the same road discussing; this every two to three weeks about making love.

Sister William, okay, I hear you Sister Grace, it's been hard: I mean to obey and submit myself to my husband; it just didn't manner. I am the woman, and I should be able to do what I want to do. Well I have and many of the other ladies have also, we have been passing this back and forward about, tell your husband this is your body and he can not have it any time; when he want to.

I am here to tell you, when church was over, and I saw this man walking down the hallway of the church, on his way to the parking lot. He pasted by me and shook my hand and said God bless you, and continued out to the parking area. I did not know that Deacon William, was about ten feet away, but Deacon William walked over to me and said, you can pull your panties up now.

He continued walking out of the door to the parking lot. Now I had just committed adultery with that man just that quick, but what made me feel so bad was I have been telling, Deacon William for a few months that I was not in the mood to make love.

I say all of that to make this point in "I Corinthian 7:1-8 Now concerning the things whereof ye wrote unto me: It is good for a man not to touch a women. Nevertheless, to avoid fornication, let every man have his own wife, and let every women have her own husband. Let the husband render unto the wife due benevolence: and likewise also the wife unto the husband.

The wife has not power of her own body, but the husband: and likewise also the husband hath not power of his own body, but the wife. Defraud you not one the other, except it be with consent for a time, that ye may give yourselves to fashing and prayer; and come together again, that Satan tempt you not for your incontinency.

But I speak this by permission, and not of commandment. For I would that all men were even as I myself. But every man hath his proper gift of God, one after this manner, and if they and another after that. I say therefore to the unmarried and widows, It is good for them if they abide even as I."

The Pastor already read this scripture to us not to be apart just for fasten and praying, but to come together again so that Satan will not tempt you. It is real sad that us women want to rule or lead when we can not and will not take care of what we have vow to do before God and our husband. To think of our husbands, who we say, that we are in love with.

We create the hardships, in our own marriages, with our selfishness, toward our husband. So, do not ask, what is the problem, with him, you have the problem, holding what is his, your body, is his he rules over it, and his body is yours and you rule over it.

You women want to rule over his body and yours, that is were the confusion comes in and that is ungodly. Okay, Okay, Okay, all right I guess you brothers had a lot to said, but we are almost out of time for this bible session. You sister has enlightened us brothers or me on the mind and set-up of our sister and women as a hold: why there are so many problems in the marriages.

Chapter 7

Husbands and Wives Must Server God

Pastor, one thing, Okay Deacon William, if women are looking at making love as a job all wives would be fired or Lay off. Woo, that's strong Deacon William; what are you saying Deacon William? That sex should truly be taken as a job. Because if we are in Christ the love we have should always make us want to be close to each other and allow us to want to make love.

Okay Sister Black, why should there be a problem making love each night. Okay Sister Black, go right head Sister William, right, your single, so right now your telling yourself my husband can have all he wants when we get married. Then months after you are married. You're telling him, is that the only thing that's on your mind.

Sister Black he is looking at you, what else should be on his mind, work? He just left work to come home to see you! To see you! Do you get it? Click! Click! Y-o-u-r the WIFE. Pastor may I make this point, go right head Sister William. I have been selfish to Deacon William's. I have asked, God to forgive me, and I asked Deacon William's to forgive me.

After all the forgiving and praying and studying God's Word, on how I was being judge by my mistreatment to Deacon William: I came to Deacon William and told him think you for not giving up on me. You see, he showed me that he was a true believer of Christ, more than I was, because he was honest; with his feeling for me and he told me what he wanted.

I would lie and did not believe in God enough or the man serving God, because of my ungodly attitude. If you say that you believe and have faith in the Word of God and you do not apply all of it, you truly do not believe.

I made myself available every night, I am ashamed to say that, because that's what the word say. Applying the word to my life. Now, I am obedience and submit to my husband, above all, I repented, and erase my sins from the lamb book of life, when it came to my husbands. Because, I freed myself from the wrong way of thinking, and now I control my husband body, and he control my body, because I make it my placed as his wife to do something to turn him on, every day he want it.

I don't want to think about him on some other women breast, just my. Well sisters and brothers we have covered a great deal this evening. Let us have prayer and go home and meditate on the words that have been shared tonight, and may be the married couples might have some discussion on their way home.

Deacon Johnson; will you lead us in prayer. "Oh most holy and all mighty God think you for this night discussion it has been enlighten to the men. But Oh Lord help the sister of the church and of the world to understand that some men are in strong need of prayer to change their ways and some women, that are out only to get what they can.

Only you God can make things happen: watch over our departure from this building and not from your present, OH God in your Son Jesus Name. Amen! Amen! Amen!"

Well you know, God works in ways that you would not believe, for the women to have been so forward. No, Pastor you must remember that these women are truly women of God, because they study the scripture and did not just read them.

Men or women can not confess that they know God's Word, and they have faith; and believe in Him: just because they are reading the bible sometime. But you see these ladies where testifying tonight, because they have found the Lord, and God's spirit made them confess their wrongdoing. Their wrongdoing was not that they did not make love to their husband, but untruthfulness in their marriage.

It would be good that they believe just by reading; but until they understand that they must study the bible. Well Pastor, we will see you next Monday. Are you not going to be at church Sunday? Good night Deacon

Grace, Sister Grace, Sister Black, Deacon Johnson, Sister Johnson, brother Earnest, Deacon Walker, Sister Walker and everyone.

Sister William, Oh God, Sister William you're something else, yes Pastor, I am; but it took me living truthfully before God's Word that made me right. I got tried of arguing about the same thing went I knew my attitude was the cause of our marital problems.

Well Sister William we are going to look forward to seeing you next Monday; Deacon William, I know you are a bless man: and I am happy too, Pastor.

"Look Diane, I didn't know that you were going to mention our earlier marital problems tonight." "I didn't plan to, but Sister Black she's not married yet, and it made us married women out to be gold diggers and that's not always true about most women.

Some of us truly love the man and want to be married to him. We just didn't know that he wanted sex more than we did. So, I think the majority of women were caught off guard. That was the reason; why I stop responding to your touch on my hip to move closer to you to make love.

I started saying we just may love last night, or am tried, or is that the only thing on your mind, your not that hot or my back hurt; I have a headache. After our conversation and I took your advice about God's Word. I really study to justify, what I had done to you was right. But the word told me that I am yours, and when something is yours, you can have it when you want and how you want, as long as, it's loving, kind, caring, and peaceful.

You know Paul, you are my lord, just like Sarah, Abraham's wife, she called him lord, and she obey and submitted to him. I know I had a problem. Obeying and Submitting, to you but; Paul I found out through my studies that I am really in love with you, and would do nothing to turn you away.

Because, of my studies, it made me understand that you were telling me the truth about my duty to you as your wife. Because, I knew that your worship and commitment to God was real, and I was not that committed to God; therefore, I was not really committed to you spiritually. I know the junk, the shouting; the anger; the unkind words; that I would say to you. All of that was to keep you from touching me until I got ready. But the Word of God and His spirit tells me that was enough, for me to do my duty as your wife.

I cried when you were not around; I didn't want you to see me. So I asked myself: why are you putting your marriage under. You are going to be judged on how you treated your husband. And the reason I know that you are a man of God. Because you stuck with me and did not beat me down; but instead encourage me to read and study God's Word for myself, and the Word will revel, itself to you: To go and asked your husband and God; for forgiveness and forgive myself.

There are so many women that think they know the word, and are in the ministers; they need to apply the word to themselves to treat their husband and children; with love and respect through their faith in God.

Husband has been stepped on far to long and the wife said; I did not think that he would have cheated on me. Well let's look at that. If your husband treated you the way that you are treating him; how would you feel about him. Now, if your husband took your car and said, you will get it back when I get ready to give it to you. Wouldn't you be angry about why he needed to take your car in the first place? Would you call friends and family: to help change your husband mind on his decisions, or go into prayer, and have God touch your husband heart to give you the car. So the car is not yours, as you thought, if someone else is controlling the use of it.

You see Paul, when some one said, that this is yours then you want it; when you want it, no condition, you want it without problems or else it is not yours; and what have been told to you was a lie. And, God dose not lie, people lie, because they are not willing to obey God.

I wanted everyone to know; Sisters William was not the only married woman that found the Lord, I did too. It was hard for me, when we started making love every single night. I didn't complain, because of my love for you and knew God for myself, at less I though I did; now I know how to take care of my responsibilities, to you for as long as I live.

It will be you to tell me, not tonight Diane, I am waiting for you to say, No. Why are you laughing Paul? I just stated everything to you; but I know you have been up front with me from the beginning. I never thought about you telling me the untruth, like I have done to you. Oh Paul, here come the children, hi," "guys where you and mother waiting long?" "Oh just about 30 minutes."

Paul will you put your hand over here, I just want to hold it, may be until we get home. Okay, everyone you know what to do when you get in the house; and I know Paul, you're going to checked all the doors and made it up stair to our bedroom. Paul I'll see you once you get there: Goodnight everyone.

Paul, I just want to know; since your getting ready for bed are you going to touch my hip tonight? Well no! Will see, I am going to touch what I want. I control your body remember get it together boy.

Morning, is the start of the new day, and everything from yesterday have hooks into this day because we went to sleep with something's that we had intended to complete, but was left unfinished. You're right about that Paul; my list that is in my head on what I need to do I may be able to complete some of these things today if time permit. I'll be in the car Diane, and we can talk some more on our way into work. Look Diane, from last night bible class there is a lot of misunderstanding in life because we do not read or study the scripture. Men and women make up their own rulers for everything to please themselves, and their rulers are so easy to break, because there is no known foundation, it is not build on God's Word.

We want to be permissive when it is, to be, right for us. And many times you are hurt from it. Studying God's Word help one to understand our purpose to God and our worship to Him. To multiple ourselves and teach our children of God's Word so they, too, will worship God.

And as we apply God's Word, we know at our end, if we have been faithful and believe in Him, and on Him, that heaven is our home. We, that are married, must not prostitute ourselves by bartering with our husband or wife, that if he or she take care of something inside or outside, of the home that you will make love, with him or her tonight.

Nor should, your husband bring you something just to make love. Your body has already been brought, through your vows; to each other: you stated vows before God, and man; on your commitment; that you made on the day of the wedding. Your bodies are God's temple it's not for sale for any reason, but men do this, because they feel, and know that it is the only way that they will be able to make love, with their wife.

We have forgotten, that your wife; have control only over the husband body, and the husband only has control over the wife body. That is the purpose of the control over the wife and husband body, because the seed is from the husband. So the wife must make sure, that the husband is the only one that is allowed, to touch her body. And the husband must make sure that the wife is the only one that is allowed, to touch his body.

Well, Paul there is one thing that I know, and it is that I got you and you have me, because I got it now, how great of a feeling it is to know the spirit of God, for yourself.

My parents talked about the family, and I had started to feel how important a female is in my life; and how it would be, being with her; looking, seeing her beauty, smelling her fragrance, and to taste her lips.

Beth, I do care for you and I know that we can come up with a school that is closer so we both can attend. I do know about this long distant dating Beth, it seen a little scary and risky to me.

I guess we can discuss this after school if you have time to do so? Sure Jerry is everything okay, yes so far, Jerry always make me nervous when he said, that we need to talk; sometimes I think that he is going to tell me that's it. Even though I know he really cares a lot for me. Oh well, let me go to class and see him after school.

I hope this is good news, may be he's not going to Yale, and we will go to a school closer to home, so we can see each other every day. This is a very long day for me today because I want to see Beth and talk about school. The time is passing slowly today that's because I want the time to speed up. Okay it almost 2:45 P.M., for the bell to ring.

Yea, all the children, from every where, poured out, of their classrooms, into the hallways and went onto the streets, everyone headed for their school bus to bring than home. I needed to make it home and started my house chores, so that I will be able to start and finish my, school homework.

One by one Franklin, Michael, and Pauline, enter the house speaking as they pass. They placed their books; in their bedrooms, and started on their chores around the house, to finish before mother and father made it home. No one said, much to any one, just busy working to finish; their work in the house. We knew that the homework from school had to be completed, before going out to play, and for sure, before we went to bed.

I had finish, with the kitchen, family room, washing dishes and vacuuming the floor. I than went up to Pauline bedroom, but she was in the bonus room cleaning and dusting. Pauline, where are you; I am in the bonus room Jerry.

I walked down the hallway to the bonus room. You know dad or mother didn't say anything about, how their bible class discussion went last night. You're right Jerry! I just thought I would ask, because they sometimes share bible class discussion with us. That's right Jerry, they didn't say anything: I just remember mother holding dad's hand in the car all the way home.

May be bible class was about being more loving come on Pauline, dad and mother act like Romeo and Julie Ate. Now, that's what? I want: for me to be in love, like father and mother. You're right Pauline, mother and father are with each other all the time like glue do you think mother and father still have sex, Pauline what do you think; how did you get here. Well, Jerry the way they move around the house and deal, with us, and work, they may not have time for it. Any way Pauline, what do you know about sex, I know more then you think, Jerry,

The other girls at school talk about it, and so, what are you saying Pauline, Oh know you better not think that of me Jerry. If I thought about it mother voice is in my head: I think mother shadow is with me all the time, okay Pauline. I just wanted to make sure that you're all right, no Jerry are you and Beth all right, the two of you kind-of-sort-of are talking about getting married.

Jerry you can tell me, is everything okay with you and Beth, what are you talking about Pauline, of course Beth and I, are okay. Well, yes, and no, we have to work out college and our dating distance. Oh is that all Jerry, that's easy; Oh ya, sure Jerry if you go to the University of Connecticut, they have a good pre-law program.

Hey, your right Pauline, you really a nice sister sometime, anything to help Jerry; remember that Jerry, in the future, that I have it together, your sister. Oh, by the way Jerry are you and Beth getting married; well Pauline I don't know. Well, I'll see; oh here comes dad and mother now! Hey, mother and father are home spouted Franklin: as he ran to the door.

He jumped up into mother arms as he doses every day, hey, hi, how is everyone: how was school today. Hey it was good that we completed our work in the house before dad and mother may it home. I finish my work dad, do you want to check it out dad; no Franklin I will see your work later when your mother and I walk through the house.

Oh, dad and mother, Pauline and I were talking, and I noticed that you and mother have not shared bible class discussion with us. You're right Jerry, on Monday, night bible discussion. Was your bible class discussion on holding hands? Wait Paul; are you going to get into detail discussion, on the class? No Diane okay, go ahead.

About married couples, and the problems that are tearing the marriage down, that causes couples to sometime divorce. Jerry there is a lot that goes into marriage, it just not love; it love to God; love of yourselves and than love to your spouse; you must be committed to God and your spouse.

The more you study God's Word and apply them earl; you can reduce the number of pitfalls; to the relationship. Women truly have a different viewpoint on marriage; than the viewpoint that men have. Mother you and dad did not always have thing together earl in your marriage.

Chapter 8

God Brings About Changes

Being honest Jerry, no, we did not, and I really feel that a larger part of our problems was because of me and my thinking and attitude. Your father is a great man to me, he stood by me when I know that I did him wrong on purpose, I was selfish.

That is the reason why it is very important that men and women be in Christ, I do not mean just going to the church building. But, in Christ, sincerely worship Him, because you need to understand His Word, and have absolute faith in Him.

And believe on Him, and in Him, that you will follow His Word, to change our ways to be godly, and have honor to the husband and wife. Before your father and I got married I felt and knew that he was a godly man.

That was one of the reasons I liked him, of course; the other was because; I love him because of his Kindness, his peace, his caring spirit and his concern for my happiness.

It was your father that showed me by his faith in God; that I must be in Christ as much or more than he was. To obey and submit to him to make our love we have real to God; to fine the true love we have for each other, without conditions.

Jerry, I think Pastor Johnson will have Rev. William teach the junior class again. He will talk to the juniors that are between the ages of 16-18, because there are young marriages and they need to know that divorce is not an option. So we must be truly sure that we understand as many of the responsibilities, within a marriage.

Jerry, most, of the young girls, all they really know is that they have this feeling, in the pit of their stomach, about how they feel about some boy. They have, know ideal of the physical, mental, emotional and spiritual impact, that is before them, at all.

That is the reason why I told Pauline, the other week, not to see this boy name Larry; because she was setting herself up for a let down; that she is not prepared to deal with at this time. But, I believe your going to get more information during the class session, Okay Jerry.

Well okay dad and mother, oh, I kind of wanted to talk to Beth about going to school here, Pauline brought this to my attention, the University of Connecticut and their pre-law program. And Jerry, you want us to do, what? If you change from Yale to the University of Connecticut, you want to know if this is going to be Okay with your mother and I, AH, yes, dad I do.

Well son, you can talk to Beth and we'll see you when you return home. O man I hope dad and mother really think about this and support my decision and the reason for this decision: To be with Beth. Is that a good enough reason to switch school? Well I m here I guess? I know that Beth and I need to discuss this to night.

Hey, Hey brother Brown, how are you doing to day I noticed you in bible class the other night and you were taken in the discussion from the brothers and sisters. Well, what did you say your name is? Oh, I didn't say, but it is Brother Harold. I m the guy that was sitting on the other side of Deacon William. Oh are you; I was married at one time then I messed up with my wife. I though that cheating was a cool thing to do, but it took me from, the lady in my life. And now I been trying for the past few years to get back together with my wife and children. I am telling you this, because I seem the way that you look at Sister Black, man. Are the two of you dating? Yes; we are Brother Harold, and hopefully the pastor will married us next June. You know Brother Harold sometime you just never know how things happen in life, or town or in the city you live in.

People from all walks of life, may cross your path; just because you need to meet them or you just need to let some people know about God; that can change us anytime if we believe. Your right Brother Brown I want you to stay with God so you can enjoy your life and your wife to be. By the way, the sisters in bible class testified about how they treated their husband. I was thinking about how I treated my wife and how through the reading and studying of God's Word; it saved me from returning to the streets. It has been, as I said before, a while since my wife and I have lived together; but I am a new man now. I am on my way over to see my wife and children and may be we can now talk about me coming home. Well Brother Harold I will keep you in prayer that God will allow you and your family to get back together.

I'll see you later Brother Harold and thank you for the words to encourage me. No, man, I thank you Brother Brown. I'll see you at church. That is why after last weeks bible class I felt that it was important for me to talk to Richard and share with him our bible discussion.

God will create the right saturation to bring you to Him. I chose to meet with Richard at the Cyhop Club, because it was close for both of us, traveling from the opposite end of town. Nikkei, Richard ex-girl friend worked at the Cyhop as a waitress. There was dancing in the back room and of course the bar was up front.

Hey, man how are you, I have not seen you in months! so what bring you to this side of town. Well Richard, like I told you over the phone I need to talk to you about something? Earnest, you just appear to be a little distant, with me ever since you joint that church. Now you're telling me that you have cleaned up your act with the ladies.

Look man, you see, Richard, I know now; because of the Word of God, that all the things that I have done to any female for the most part was wrong. But you see Richard, it was more than for me to just joint the church: I had to ask God to forgive me and I repented for my sins. Then, I had to go to all the ladies that I knew, and ask each of them; that I have been with, to forgive me.

So, Earnest, this should make everything now okay, with God, because you have done that. Yes Richard, this is just a recovery from what I have done and now as I study God's Word and attend bible class, and Sunday school to help me better understand God's Word, to grow strong in the Lord.

I have understood more now, about what my father and mother, have been trying to tell me for years. Okay, Earnest now here we are at the bar and you see that find lady in the middle of the bar. What are you feeling right now? Okay, Okay, Richard, let me explain something, no: What are your feeling right now? Earnest! Okay! Yes, I would love to go over to her and talk, but because I have understood the value of being, with Christ Jesus: I would go over to her, but to tell her about the Lord and not try to get over on her just to get her in bed.

Do you hear yourself Earnest: the man that women asked other men about, just to get him in bed; and you're telling me, that you just let all of that good stuff slide through your finger, just like that.

Man, let me tell you something, give me your telephone book, wait, wait, Richard. There are women that are attracted to you just like the ones that where attracted to me. But that's in the pass now: Well it may be in the past for you, but not for me Earnest. I am going to talk to that lady at the bar. You just watch me Earnest.

Okay Richard, I don't think you want to talk to her man.

I'll be right back Richard I just need to make a phone call to Sister Black. You mean Carol, ya, Sister Black, since, when have you started back seeing Carol just about nine months ago? What happen that you revived that dead relationship? Well I started attending bible class about a year ago and would you know it, Sister Black was there.

Wait, didn't you know that she was a member of this church, no? So I asked her how long was she a member, she, said about two years since we stop seeing each other. Earnest, I don't know why you stop seeing Carol in the first place; she was real good for you. Yea, wasn't she! But I just wanted to see more women.

So what real happen that make you change. I was over my sister and brother-in-law home playing with my nephew and nice. My sister asked me, when was I going to get married, and have my own family. She said, Earnest your really great with the children. You need your own, by the way what happen to Chesmile or the other one Carol.

I told her well I didn't think they were for me. Well you know the question; how do you know, that they are not the one for you: when the only think that you are doing, is hop-skip and jumping around to all the ladies.

Look, Earnest you are not going to be able to have all the women in the world, a few billion, you are going to miss some or dried without having them. But you can enjoy one women for the rest of your life, and make love went you want to, and then have some children and enjoy, your wife, everyday and not just on the weekends or once a month.

Earnest, women have their issue, too, but Peter, I love him and I try to be there for him, because everything I do impact Peter and the children. I know you have heard stories from other married men like brother Windy about, how he was with some other women, because his wife did not make herself available to make love.

So, Richard all that conversation, with Mary just stayed, with me for months. So, after going to bible class for months, and not real saying anything, to Sister Black. One night after bible class I asked her if we could talk, she said yes. Earnest, I know what she did; I bet she put her hands, on her hips and read you.

No, she was receptive, she just said okay Earnest we can talk where. I said let's stop at the coffeehouse down on fifth street: she agreed, I arrived before Sister Black, and was sitting waiting to see if she was going to come in.

Sister Black waited one minute, why are you calling her sister Black, because that is her name. No, man, her name is Carol, but Richard she is Sister Black to me now, because she is saved. She really is into God's Word; and I respect her as a sister in Christ. Hey, man, are you all right; because you, and this entire sister stuff, and church, and bible class are you touched? Yes, Richard, I am touched by the Word of God, and I have not felt like this every in my live.

Okay, man now what happen with Carol, my bag, Sister Black, she arrived and the waitress bought her over to the table, where I was seated. I said, hi, Sister Black, she said oh, hi, Brother Brown, you look a little surprise Brother Brown, like I was not going to come. Well, to be honest, I didn't think you where going to show up, because of the last words that we had.

Well, Brother Brown, I was really upset with you, because you told me that you just wanted to be, with me, then I saw you, and Chesmile. Oh, Man, is that, when Sister Black poured some hot coffee on you, no Richard, Sister Black, really, I think changed from the way that she was. So, Richard that's when, Sister Black and I began talking about everything. I have asked, Sister Black to forgive me, for all that I have done to her the last time we where dating. About three months later I asked Sister Black to married me. Wow! Earnest, now you're going to get married, yes, I shared my true feeling, with Sister Black and I felt that she has shared her feeling with me.

But, you have just been talking for nine months or is this just to get her in bed. No, I having been with anyone that way since I have turn my life over to Jesus. But, don't you tell me that you have not touch anyone in over a year an half man, who do you think I am, am your friend and I know you Earnest.

Yes, you do, and I have change Richard. Anyhow, Sister Black, and I will be married in six months, I want you to be my best man. Now, let me make this phone call to Sister Black, and tell her that I spoke to you and by the way; would you like to come to the church with me this Sunday. AH, let me think about it. But, right now, I am going to talk to this lady at the bar.

Oh, man that lady shoulder and back look like a man that's a guy, dressed up like a women. She/he turned as Richard drew near, let me keep walking and go over to Nikkie.

Look, Nikkie, hi, I know I have not seen you in months, but I need a favor right now from you okay. What is it Richard lean over and kiss me, you want me to kiss you and it's been, Nikkie was breathless, oh Richard it's been a long time, let me caught my breath.

Richard, why don't we take this to a better place then this, like your place: well Nikkie your right, let me tell Earnest that I am going; okay Richard, come right back dear, your honey is waiting. Oh Earnest I got to go Nikkie is waiting on me, and by the way that lady is a man. Wait Richard: What you are planning to do is called fornication that is a sin?

What you need to understand Richard is that man was created in the image of God and woman represent the church, the creation from the bone of man. God commanded; that men and women be fruitful, and multiples, and worship Him (God). We are to create others like ourselves from male and female unite, **but we must be married first before we start making love.**

There is a bond that is created between male and female that is directed by God. The man must seek after God, obey God, worship God, pray to God and receive God's direction on all things.

Likewise, so must the woman do the same unto God and look to her husband; because God created him first and the women was created for the man. With husband and wife relationship, they know how to turn to God for all things.

Husband and wives must respect, like, love, communicate; to each other on every issues big or small, about children, sex, romance, intimacy, money, how to spend money and what things they should buy.

In-law's, out-law's, friends, relatives, associates at work, church issues, bible discussion, World events, your best friend; do not come before your spouse. Your wife or husband (male and Female only) should be your" Best Friend" outside of Jesus Christ. You should be able to talk about anything, and everything; with your spouse and not hear about it outside of the home: or be shoot down or be put down, about your subject matter, from your spouse.

Richard if you are planing to get back with Nikkie, why not due it the right way through the word? You do not need to go to bed to prove anything to each other about how you feel. I am not telling you that it is going to be easy, but it will be the right thing to do for your soul salvation. Our focus should be on haven, and truly enjoy our time here on earth before we die. I know that I may be coming down on you a little hard Richard but I want you to truly get the chance to by happy with your life.

It is not about having ladies name in your phone book, but it is about having the true name of our creator in our hearts. Okay Brother Brown if I do this thing that your talking about, like go to church with you this Sunday and attend bible class how will that help me. I am so glad that you ask. When you believe in the Lord Jesus Christ, that he was born, die on the cross, and on the third day he got up with all power given unto Him. Then you are a believer of God's Word, now to help you grow in God's Word you need to study the Word of God. Richard as you study God's Word, there will be times; that may appear to be difficult, that is when you go into prayer, because you just can't figure out how to solve this problem. I am not telling you Richard that this is going to be a cake walk, but I am telling you that this will be the walk that you would want to have for your life. I truly am a witness of God's work and power, how he has change me to whom I am now. I like that; because now I can speak and know that it is the truth. All of this is good stuff Brother Earnest, but to be honest I am just a little scary about all this stuff that you are dumping on me right now. Remember man you been doing this stuff for about two years now and your telling me these things, like I am going to be fix right now. Should you believe, you would be fix right now. I know that this is a journey and I am still traveling Richard, every one that fellow Jesus Christ is traveling to make it into heaven.

Will you come and joint us on this journey and have your spirit lifted up to enjoy life as it was met to be.

Again, you and Nikkie are friends that can date (male and female Relationship couples only) make sure that, that her spirit is in tune with yours; in order to feel that this is the choice God has setup for you. So that your children if God bless you with them; you would want then to serve God. If you serve God; or if you are not servicing God: then you need to find out, how to serve Him: in order that you would learn of Him, so that you will grow, based on your willingness to serve God.

It is a lot Richard; and I guess I can go on for days talking about God. All the father and mother (male and female) who are teaches their children that this is what God want as a family. And any other form of a relationship of male and male or female and female is an abomination (a Sin). Because, if you are committing an abomination you are not obeying God's command of being fruitful and you can not multiples in that form of a relationship to have children. The gay and lesbian individuals where birth from a male and female couple.

Yea, I know Brother Brown because I think men, may be thinking, that being, with another man will give them endless sex or that they can buy a male prostitute and be fulfill sexually. But the ultimate cost is damnation from God; in this sinful life style; that you think that, it will be; blessed by God. However, women thinking now they are safe, because they don't need to be concern about men dumping then for another women.

Or, even, getting pregnant any more. Because, a women is not going to treat her, the way that a man would. And she another woman and women know how to treat each other and men don't. But this type of thinking mislead so many women that fall into this sinful way; thinking that they can get out of this any time that they wanted too.

But, the ultimate cost is damnation from God, in this sinful life style. They think it is blessed by God: but until men and women that have selected this type of life style; come to God, and must repent for their wicked ways. They will never leave or be able to get out of that sinful life style; without God. You see Brother Brown I know some things that's in the bible, and you are right I will be there on Sunday, man. You're all right Brother even though you messed up my play you're still all right with me.

This type of home setting will teach adopted children, that it is okay for male and male, or female and female to be together sexual this may confuse those children; because the norm (male and female) will be looked at as abnormal. Richard here are the scripture; "Leviticus 18:22" Thou shalt not lie with mankind, as with womankind: it is abomination. "

"Romans 1:24-32, Wherefore God also gave them up to uncleanness through the lusts of their own hearts, to dishonor their own bodies between themselves: Who changed the truth of God onto a lie, and worshipped and served the creature more than the Creator, Who is blessed forever.

Amen. For this cause God gave them up unto vile affections: for even their women did change the natural use into that which is against nature. And likewise also the men, leaving the natural use of the woman; burned in their lust one toward another; men with men working that which is unseemly, and receiving in them that recompense of their error, which was meet.

And even as they did not like to retain God in their knowledge, God gave them over to a reprobate mind, to do those things which are not convenient. Being filled with all un-righteousness, fornication, wickedness, covetousness, maliciousness: full of envy, murder, debate, deceit, and malignity: whisper, backbiters, haters of God, despite, proud, boasters, inventors of evil things, disobedient to parents. Without understanding, covenant breakers, without natural affection, implacable, unmerciful. Who knowing the judgment of God, that they which commit such things are worthy of death, not only do the same, but have pleasure in them that do them."

"Genesis 18:20-27 And the Lord said, Because the cry of Sodom and Go-mor'rah is great, and because their sin is very grievous. I will go down now, and see whether they have done altogether according to the cry of it, which is come unto me and if not, I will know.

And the men turned their faces from thence, and went toward Sodom: but Abraham stood yet before the Lord. And Abraham drew near, and said, Wilt thou also destroy the righteous with the wicked?

Peradventure there be fifty righteous within the city: wilt thou also destroy and not spare the place for the fifty righteous that are therein?

That be far from thee to do after this manner, to slay the righteous with the wicked: and that the righteous should be as the wicked, that be far from thee: shall not the Judge of all the earth do right?

And the Lord said, If I find in Sodom fifty righteous within the city, then I will spare all the place for their sakes. And Abraham answered and said, Behold now, I have taken upon me speak unto the Lord, which am but dust and ashes: Peradventure there shall lack five of the fifty? And he said, If I find there forty and five, I will not destroy it.

And he spoke unto him yet again, and said, Peradventure there shall be forty found there, And he said, I will not do it for forty's sake." "Genesis 19:1-28 And there came two angels to Sodom at even; and Lot sat in the gate of Sodom: and Lot seeing them rose up to meet them; and he bowed himself with his face toward the ground;

And he said, Behold now, my lords, turn in, I pray you, into your servant's house, and tarry all night, and wash your feet, and ye shall rise up early, and go on your ways. And they said, Nay; but we will abide in the street all night. And he pressed upon them greatly; and they turned in unto him, and entered into his house; and he made them a feast, and they did eat.

But before they lay down, the men of the city, even the men of Sodom, compassed the house round, both old and young, all the people from every quarter: And they called unto Lot, and said unto him, Where are the men which came in to thee this night? Bring them out unto us, that we may know them.

And Lot went out at the door unto them, and shut the door after him, And said, I pray you, brethren, do not so wickedly, Behold now, I have two daughters which have not known man; let me, I pray you, bring them out unto you, and do ye to them as is good in your eyes: only unto these men do nothing; for therefore came they under the shadow of my roof.

And they said, again, This one fellow came in to sojourn, and he will be a judge: now will we deal worse with thee, than with them. And they pressed sore upon the man, even Lot, and came near to break the door. But the men put forth their hand, and pulled Lot into the house to them, and shut to the door. And they smote the men that were at the door of the house with blindness, both small and great: so that they wearied themselves to find the door.

And the men said unto Lot, Hast thou here any besides? Son in law, and thy sons, and thy daughters, and whatsoever thou hast in the city, bring them out of this place. For we will destroy this place because the cry of them is waxen great before the face of the Lord; and the Lord hath sent us to destroy it.

And Lot went out, and spake unto his sons in law, which married his daughters, and said, Up, get you out of this place; for the Lord will destroy this city. But he seem as one that mocked unto his son in law. And when the morning arose, then the angels hastened Lot, saying, Arise, take thy wife, and thy two daughters, which are here; lest thou be consumed in the iniquity of the city.

The sun was risen upon the earth when Lot entered into Zoar. Then the Lord rained upon Sodom and upon Go-mor'-rah brimstone and fire from the Lord out of heaven; And he overthrew those cities, and all the plain, and all the inhabitants of the cities, and that which grew upon the ground.

But his wife looked back from behind him, and she became a pillar of salt. And Abraham got up early in the morning to the place where he stood before the Lord: And he looked toward Sodom and Go-mor'-rah, and toward all the land of the plain, and beheld, and, lo, the smoke of the country went up as the smoke of a furnace."

Chapter 9

How to Correct Your Marriage

I'll see Richard, hey Brother Brown thanks for the bible class and helping me understand that my thinking was not on track. Let me go and tell Nikkie that we should be going to church and not up to the bedroom. I am going to see if Nikkie will come with me to church on Sunday. By Richard, see later Brother Brown, oh by the way, yes I'll be your best man, thanks.

Wait one minute, I though you forgot about me and went home Richard and you mean to tell me, that you have been talking to Earnest about what? No, here I am ready and waiting on you and you stood me up to talk to Earnest. No that's not it Nikkie, what Brother Brown had to tell me was very important for my life, no for our life. Well what do you mean our life? Look Nikkie I know that it going to sound stupid but do you want to go to heaven when you die. Well yes Richard I am a good person you know that and you missed that, talking to Earnest in stayed of taken care of this stuff. Why are you talking about heaven now Richard? Because I want to attend church and I want you to come with me. Wait just one minute. You let this man that had all the women talked you into going to church this man even have game on you. What do I look like walking into church, I don't know Richard? Do I need to have on something yes, that will cover you and a little long then that dress? So, when did you tell Earnest; that we will come, this Sunday? Don't forget to pick me up Richard, I'll be waiting to here of a better reason if you don't pick me up. Nikkie, I'll see you later and we can talk while we are having dinner.

You know Diane I feel that the pastor is going to talk about where our strengthen is, and how it comes from the Lord; and the man uses his strength from God; to direct his family as he provide for them from God's blessing. The woman user her strength to keep her family intact, warm, loving, kind, and making provision for her husband who provide for the family.

The storm may come, but the husband and wife who knows God: will pray to Him when times are good and when there are trouble times; to strengthen their family to survive, theses storms.

When you look at the man and the woman, God made them, with everything that is needed; that the man can be satisfy, by the woman, and the woman is satisfy by the man, spiritually, emotionally and sexual. Take a look at these scriptures "Husbands and Wives-I Peter 3:1-8 Likewise, ye wives, be in subjection to your own husband; that, if any obey not the word, they also may without the word be won by the conversation of the wives; While they behold your chaste conversation coupled with fear. Whose adorning let it not be that outward adorning of plaiting or of putting on of apparel; But let it be the hidden man of the heart, in that which is not corruptible, even the ornament of a meek and quiet spirit, which is in the sight of God of great price. For after this manner in the old time the holy women also, who trusted in God, adorned themselves, being in subjection unto their own husbands: Even as Sara obeyed Abraham, calling him lord: whose daughters ye are, as long as ye do well, and are not afraid with any amazement.

Likewise, you husbands, dwell with them according to knowledge, giving honour unto the wife, as unto the weaker vessel, and as being heirs together of the grace of life; that your prayers be not hindered. Finally, be you all of one mind, having compassion one of another, love as brethren, be pitiful, be courteous."

"Ephesians 5:21-33 Submitting, yourselves one to another in the fear of God. Wives, submit yourselves unto your own husbands, as unto the Lord. For the husband is the head of the wife, even as Christ is the head of the church: and he is the saviour of the body. Therefore as the church is subject unto Christ, so let the wives be to their own husbands in everything.

Husbands, love your wives, even as Christ also loved the church, and gave himself for it; That he might sanctify and cleanse it with the washing of water by the word. That he might present it to himself a glorious church not having spot, or wrinkle, or any such thing; but that it should be holy and without blemish.

So ought men to love their wives as their own bodies. He that loveth his wife loveth himself. For no men ever yet hated his own flesh; but nourisheth and cherisheth it, even as the Lord the church: For we are members of his body, of his flesh, and of his bones.

For this cause shall a man leave his father and mother, and they two shall be one flesh. This is a great mystery: but I speak concerning Christ and the church. Nevertheless let every one of you in particular so love his wife even as himself; and the wife see that she reverence her husband."

The unmarried states is good; but Christian marriage is for the purpose of avoiding fornication and establishing a mutually satisfactory monogamous relationship; in which both partners (male and female, husband and wife) express full bodily powers in normal satisfactory physical union.

Many time men are out of control, and they run after every female, that they meet, because of their sexual desire. As we think about God, we need to make sure that you're under His direction in order that; everything is done decent and in order. So, adultery, fornicator, homosexual, lesbian, whomorger are not under God's covenant. God wanted us to think wisely about the things that we planed to do.

We are upset, because things have not worked out, the way we wanted them to; and our wife or husband has not agreed with the way that we wanted to do things in the home. Therefore, we become upset, angry, use wrong words, or the choice of words we use, and call each other out of their name.

Our relationship with Christ; teachers us to be loving, kindhearted, and to keep peace with one another. We only need to present something to our spouse, no brewer beating them, with other information on the subject. Let, them, go unto God in pray, about what decision our spouse may make, on things we feel are important. Paul this is what I am talking about, the importance of love as it is pointed out in the scripture.

"Love Each Other-I John 3:11-24 For this is the message that ye heard from the beginning that we should love one another.

Not as Cain, who was of that wicked one, and slew his brother. And wherefore slew he him? Because his own works were evil, and his brother's righteous.

Marvel not, my brethren, if the world hate you. We know that we have passed from death unto life, because we love the brethren. He that loveth not his brother abideth in death. Whosoever hate his brother is a murderer: and ye know that no murderer hath eternal life abiding in him.

Hereby perceive we the love of God, because he laid down his life for us: and we ought to lay down our lives for the brethren.

But who so have this world's good, and seeth his brother have need, and shutteth up his bowels of compassion from him, how dwelleth the love of God in him?

My little children, let us not love in word, neither in tongue; but in deed and in truth. And hereby we know that we are of the truth, and shall assure our hearts before him. For if our heart condem us, God is greater than our heart, and knoweth all things.

Beloved, if our heart condem us not, then have we confidence toward God. And whatsoever we ask, we receive of him, because we keep his commandments, and do those things that are pleasing in his sight.

And this is his commandment. That we should believe on the name of his Son Jesus Christ, and love one another, as he gave us commandment. And he that keep his commandments dwelleth in him, and he in him; And hereby we know that he abideth in us, by the Spirit which he hath given us."

Your husband and wives are going to make mistake, errors, spend too much money, making quick decision on things. Just talk to him or her, to gain an understanding for that decision, but discuss the issue with respect one to the other.

The union of the man and women is the strongest relationship on earth in the eyes of God. For the wife receives the care, protection, direction, love, children, support, respect and kindness from her husband and the husband receives her love, care, warmth, children, kindness, respect and support from the wife.

Because the male and female are able to have children together, this show us the importance of man and woman development: out of such a relationship; makes this a strong unit, for future generation that they thoughts are to meet the end result (Happiness, and the Kingdom of God). God may not gives us what we desire, at this moment and time, so we become displease disappointed, and even angry; we don't want to wait on God, but we need to.

We must understand that God is in control of all things, at all times, and our faith will be tested daily. So we must renew our faith each day, too withstand our test, for the day. Your wife can help by examining herself as she pray for you and her to be clean and pure, before God.

The husband can help by examining himself, as he pray, for you and him to be clean and pure, before God. We must ask God's forgiveness of our sins, and try not to repeat those sins, but to go forward to clean up our house, repent (our bodies) that they will be sacrifice unto God, as we pray, for ourselves and others.

We can not come before God, without asking Him, to forgive us, of our sins to receive His blessing.

We must repent of our sins before God. Else, we will die in sin. God knows our mind and if we think that we can speech words: without the words coming from a humble heart, and mind, you would have fooled yourself; with your prayers.

Now let me share these scripture with you Diane; "Truth and Love-II John 1:3-11 Grace be with you, mercy, and peace, from God the Father, and from the Lord Jesus Christ, the Son of the Father, in truth and love. I rejoiced greatly that I found of thy children walking in truth, as we have received a commandment from the Father.

And now; I beseech thee, lady, not as though I wrote a new commandment unto thee, but that which we had from the beginning, that we love one another. And this is love that we walk after his commandments. This is the commandment, That, as ye have heard from the beginning, ye should walk in it.

For many deceivers are entered into the world, who confess not that Jesus Christ is come in the flesh.

This is a deceiver and an antichrist. Look to yourselves, that we lose not those things, which we have wrought, but that we receive a full reward.

Whosoever transgresseth, and abideth not in the doctrine of Christ, hath not God. He that abideth in the doctrine of Christ, he hath both the Father and the Son.

If there come any unto you, and bring not this doctrine, receive him not into your house, neither bid him God speed: For he that biddeth him God speed is partaker of his evil deeds."

Put, God in your mind (heart), daily as he has awaking you with thanksgiving. Your love for your spouse, through God's blessing, will let you know that you are so much a part of Him, and He's of you, that it hurts to be along, without each other through the night and day.

There is no one that can or will replace such a spouse for you in Christ. So enjoy, everyday, with your spouse (male and female relationship only), to get all the gusto that you deserve. It is as important for women to disclose many of her problems that may help the man they are planing to married; as well as the man that is thinking of you.

Share with him or her, if there was a rape, other childhood problems, your mother with other men after your mother divorce; your father that cause problems for you, sex abuse by a family member or a friend when you were young. And other things that may have happen in the past, drugs, alcohol, prostitution, lesbians, being gate; this may help that person you are wanting to married, as you share some truthful things in your life.

And the reason for sharing: is that there should be some understanding as to who you are, if a event comes up after your married; that now you can both work on the problem together. It should reduce many problems; sure as sexual issue, or other issue, that may take the marital relationship on a journey: that might end up in divorce.

We all have some type of issues, but are these issues going to cause major problems, for your spouse. Would your spouse be able to handle your issues? Men and women might come out of their hang ups, if another male or female is able to talk to them; if they are aware of their saturation. A lack of confidence may be present, trying to discuss it, but with a friends it may help, with some of your problems before you married.

Secrets will impact the marriage and other problems, lies, money, and sexual issues. If you want your marriage to work, than you must work hard at it, without excuses to make it work. We have taken too many things for granted and we are saying that my wife is all right, my husband is all right. But, we do not look into; what might be the feelings of the other person we are in love with, to determine the type of problems they might be having.

The problem; I may think is not important, and just over looking it, because: what I am doing is far more important than what my wife or husband has as a problem. We need to understand the important of the earthly issue in our life; to reach for the heavenly answer from heaven we should make sure, we are in Christ.

How, important is God in our life, for love, for blessing, for peace, for happiness, for the strengthen of our faith; and too strengthen our believe. The education from the earthly church helps us to search for the heavenly answers, with Christ.

So, let us apply the scriptures to our life; not just for the benefit of heaven, but for the joy that we receive here on earth every day, with our husbands, wife, children, family and friends. The earthly church, teach us about the love that we need to have; to our family members, and to share it with all others. Let's not forget, our spouses, they are the major character; in God's plan.

Chapter 10

God's Word Will Always Hold True

This is another Sunday morning and we are on our way to church and it look like we are going to arrive early to attend Sunday school. We know that the Pastor, will bring forth the word, helping us to understand that it dose not matter; what problems you may have, God will see you through, what every your problems are.

Good morning saints, it has been another week with it's situation for they that believe shell be saved. I noticed that we have some visitor with us this morning welcome to every one. Now we need to prayer, for everyone. "Dear Lord as you look down on us last night and touch us this morning with life being given to us one more time. Father we ask that your word be heard this day that any one that must come unto you; let your word touch me, as it is delivered to this waiting congregation. View their life and as they wait for your return: I asked these blessing in your Son Jesus name and everyone said. Amen! Amen! And Amen!"

Let us read from the book of "I Peter 1: 13-25 My theme is; Chosen to live a Holy Life.

Wherefore gird up the loins of your mind, be sober, and hope to the end for the grace that is to be brought unto you at the revelation of Jesus Christ. As obedient children, not fashioning yourselves according to the former lusts in your ignorance: But as he which hath called you is holy, so be ye holy in all manner of conversations.

Because it is written, Be ye holy: for I am holy.

And if you call on the Father, who without respect of persons judgeth according to every man's work, pass the time of your sojourning here in fear: For as much as you know that ye were not redeemed with corruptible things, as silver and gold from your vain conversation received by tradition from your fathers;

But with the precious blood of Christ, as of a lamb without blemish and without spot: Who verily was foreordained before the foundation of the world, but was manifest in these last times for you. Who by him do believe in God, that raised him up from the dead, and gave him glory; that your faith and hope might be in God.

Seeing you have purified your souls in obeying the truth through the Spirit unto unfeigned love of the brethren, see that ye love one another with a pure heart fervently: Being born again, not of corruptible seed, but of incorruptible, by the word of God, which liveth and abideth for ever.

For all flesh is as grass, and all the glory of man as the flower of grass. The grass withereth, and the flower, thereof fall away: But the word of the Lord endureth for ever. And this is the word which by the gospel is preached unto you."

Chosen to live a Holy Life;

"Let all so distinguished, gird up the loins of their minds. You have a journey, a race to run, a warfare to accomplish, and a great work to do. As the traveler, the racer, the warrior, and the laborer, gathered in their long and loose garments, that they might be ready in their business, so do you by your minds and affections.

Live Holy;

Be sober, be vigilant against, all spiritual dangers and enemies, and be temperate in recreation, business, and all behavior; be sober-minded in opinion, as well as in practice, and humble in your judgment of yourselves.

And hope perfectly, trust, without doubting, in that grace now offered by the gospel.

Live Holy;

A strong and perfect trust in the grace of God is very consistent with our best endeavors in our duty; we must hope perfectly, yet gird up our loins, and address ourselves vigorously to the work we have to do, encouraging ourselves from the grace of Jesus Christ.

You chosen to live a Holy Life;

The children of God ought to prove themselves by their obedience to God. The best of them have had their times of lust and ignorance; the time has been, when the scheme of their lives; their way and fashion, was, to accommodate and gratify earthly desires and appetites, being ignorant of God and themselves, of Christ and the gospel.

You must Live Holy;

Holiness is the desire and duty of every Christian. It must be universal; in all affairs, in every condition, towards all people. We must especially watch and pray against the sin to which we are inclined. As God is holy: we must imitate Him, though we can never equal Him.

Be Holy;

He is perfectly, unchangeably, eternally holy; and the consideration of the holiness of God should oblige us to the highest degrees of holiness we can attain. The Word of God; is the surely the rule for Christian life, and by this rule we are commanded to be holy every way.

Live Holy;

It is unquestionably among those who profess themselves to be the people of God, some who are indeed His children, and bear His image both in their hearts and in their lives. This impression of holiness is on their souls and conversation; but with the most, a name and form of godliness are all they have for religion.

You must chose to Live Holy;

And the judgment of God will be without respect of persons, according to every man's work. Faith, works evidence whether we have complied with our visiting them with corrections. Then let Christians not doubt God's faithfulness to His promises, nor give way to enslaving the dread of His wrath: but being watchful lest they dishonor God and incur His rebukes, lest they fall into temptation and disgrace their profession.

The consideration of our redemption ought to be a constant and powerful inducement to holiness and the fear of God. Silver and gold, and things of this world, often are snares, temptations, and hinder to salvation, but can by no means purchase or procure salvation.

Be Holy;

The redemption of man is real, we are bought with a price, and the price is equal to the purchase, for it is the precious blood of Christ. A person without blemish and without spot, whom the paschal lamb represented, and an infinite person, being the Son of God, one with the another.

Be Holy;

And the design of Christ in shedding His most precious blood, was, to redeem us, not only from eternal misery hereafter, but from a vain conversation in this world. Not only openly wicked, but also unprofitable conversation is highly dangerous, though it may plead antiquity and custom in its defense; nor is it wise to resolve, I will live and die in such a way, because my forefathers did so.

Be Holy;

The redeemer is further described, as one ordained before the foundation of the world, but He was manifested to be that Redeemer by His birth. By His Father's testimony, and His own works, especially His resurrection from the dead, when He was invested with all power in heaven and earth, and glorified with that glory which He had with God before the world was.

Jesus walked on this earth for thirty-three years and was preaching and healing people for three years and Jesus: was nailed to that cross for your sins and mind He had the blood and water that ran down His side.

And the Roman solider gave Jesus some vinegar in a sprang attached to the spear to drink, but Jesus refuse to drink it. And——— a-bout the—nine—hour Jesus——- cried out with—in a-loud—voice, saying E'li,E'li, la'ma sa-bach'tha-ni? And———that is to say, My God, my God, why——-hast—thou—forsaken——-me?

Then He hung His head and dried. He was placed in another man tomb and say there all day Friday and all night, all day Saturday, and than early——,early—! On the third day, Sunday morning Jesus go up and said, all power that's been given unto me as he stood on the land and the sea." Amen—Amen-Amen.

Some church members began to shout, because of the joy they knew in Jesus, and they knew that Jesus, have saw them through many hard times and tribulation. Do you know Him, do you want to know Him, the doors of the church are open (meaning come and be a member of the church).

You could join by letter, water baptism or Christian experience: is there one that will take the right hand of fellowship today. The deacons were standing in front, next to the pull pit with out reached hands for any new members. A few men and women jointed the church; Brother Brown do you see what I see? Yes I do Sister Black. What did you say to Nikkie and Richard? I just shared the word with Richard about what he and Nikkie were getting ready to do was sinful? The pastor, open the doors, of the church it appeared, just for Richard and Nikkie. Now, the Pastor is going to say the benediction. Paul that was a beautiful message; and a number of people enjoyed it as well. Yes, I saw Jerry and Beth talking to their friends in the back of the church. Let's get the children together and get ready to head for home. Diane, Sister William is tying to get your attention, okay Paul let me see what she wants, I'll be right back. Jerry, yes dad do your know where your brothers and sister are? Well not at this moment dad, but I'll look for then oh dad they're out in the parking lot. Okay Jerry, thank you.

All right is every one in? Yes were all here and ready to head for home and get some thing to eat, right Franklin. Right dad. Sunday afternoon, are slow and quiet, no one is rushing on the street to go anywhere. It's just like that on Sunday, I guess to get you ready for school on Monday. But it's also a good day for going to the park, or the movies and finish homework before school. The hours of the day have come and it was another Monday night for bible class and we are going to attend another class session on the bible. Every one races to the car, dad said, Franklin you and Michael cools your jets, we will get to class on-time in-time, okay fellows.

As we arrival at the church, and enter the classroom, where the children attended their class; the Pastor was waiting on us to enter the classroom, in order to begin from where we left off on last week. The Pastor said, okay, every one, Deacon Walker will let us in prayer, "Dear God thank you for another week and another day that you made it possible for all of us to return to this class for more spiritual education, and knowledge of your word.

We asked that you bless Pastor Johnson and his family and all the children, sister's and brothers, of this church in Jesus name. Amen! Amen! Amen!" Thank you, for that prayer, Deacon Walker. Last week, when we stopped; Sister Walker was speaking or Sister William. Did you want to pick up from what you where speaking about on last week Sister Walker? AH, yes Pastor. I wanted to say that it is not easy being married when you do not want to do the right things.

Since, I have stop my excuses, for not wanting to make love or be intimate; it is almost like I no longer have excuses or tell lies or have excuses about other things.

I owe all of this to God: He has strength me and has given me a great love, for my husband Deacon Walker, family, friends and other people. I stay in prayer, because I needed it and that is the reason I can stand here tonight, because of the love that God has given me.

One more thing, I wanted to say, sex is not the problem, nor is money, it is, because, you do not want, to love, and do not have a God fearing attitude, that is keeping you from loving your spouse and every one else.

Start, with yourself ladies, to love your husbands and I truly believe once you apply God's Word, to your life you will not have a need; to block making love, and learn to be truthful about everything, life will blossom with God's grace.

Okay, now I would like to read these two scripture. Proverbs 31:10-31" Who can find a virtuous woman? For her price is far above rubies. The heart of her husband doth safely trust in her, so that he shall have no need of spoil. She will do him good and not evil all the days of her life. She seek wool, and flax, and worketh willingly with her hands.

She is like the merchant ships; she brineth her food from afar. She rise also while it is yet night, and giveth meat to her household, and a portion to her maidens. She consider a field and buy it: with the fruit of her hands she planteth a vineyard.

She gird her loins with strength, and strengtheneth her arms. She perceive that her merchandise is good: her candle goeth not out by night. She lay her hands to the spindle, and her hands hold the distaff. She stretch out her hand to the poor; yea, she reacheth forth her hands to the needy.

She is not afraid of the snow for her household: for all her household are clothed with scarlet. She make herself coverings of tapestry; her clothing is silk and purple. Her husband is known in the gates, when he sitteth among the elders of the land. She make fine linen, and selleth it; and delivereth girdles unto the merchant.

Strength and honor are her clothing; and she shall rejoice in time to come.

She open her mouth with wisdom and in her tongue is the law of kindness. She look well to the ways of her household, and eat not the bread of idleness. Her children arise up, and call her blessed; her husband also, and her praiseth her.

Many daughters have done virtuously, but thou excellent them all. Favor is deceitful, and beauty is vain: but a woman that feareth the Lord, shall be praised. Giver her of the fruit of her hands; and let her own works praise her in the gates."

"Ephesians 5:20-33" Giving thanks always for all things unto God and the Father in the name of our Lord Jesus Christ; Submitting yourselves one to another in the fear of God. Wives, submit yourselves unto your own husbands, as unto the Lord. For the husband is the head of the wife, even as Christ is the head of the church: and he is the Saviour of the body.

Therefore as the church is subject unto Christ, so let the wives be to their own husbands in everything. Husband, love your wives, even as Christ also loved the church, and gave himself for it; That he might sanctify and cleanse it with the washing of water by the word, That he might present it to himself a glorious church, not having spot, or wrinkle, or any such thing; but that it should be holy and without blemish. So ought men to love their wives as their own bodies. He that loveth his wife loveth himself. For no man ever yet hated his own flesh; but nourisheth and cherisheth it, even as the Lord the church: For we are members of his body, of his flesh, and of his bones.

For this cause shall a man leave his father and mother, and shall be joined unto his wife, and they two shall be one flesh.

This is a great mystery: but I speak concering Christ and the church. Nevertheless let every one of you in particular so love his wife even as himself; and the wife see that she reverence her husband."

"An example from Marriage-Romans 7:1-6 Know you not, brethren, (for I speak to them that know the law,) how that the law hath dominion over a man as long as he liveth? For the woman which hath an husband is bound by the law to her husband so long as he liveth; but if the husband be dead, she is loosed from the law of her husband.

So then if, while her husband liveth, she be married to another man, she shall be called an adulteress: but if her husband be dead, she is free from that law; so that she is no adulteress, though she be married to another man. Wherefore, my brethren, ye also become dead to the law by the body of Christ; that ye should be married to another, even to him who is raised from the dead, that we should bring forth fruit unto God.

For when we were in the flesh, the motions of sins, which were by the law, did work in our members to bring forth fruit unto death. But now we are delivered from the law, that being dead wherein we were held; that we should serve in newness of spirit, and not in the oldness of the letter."

Chapter 11

Your Faith Will Allow God to Come Through For You

You see; I am glad that Sister Walker, Sister William and Sister Grace shared with us on last week, what they had to do, for their marriage. To do the right thing before God, and how the husbands acted by going to God, because their wives were not doing everything in regard to their bodies, they also, needed to submit to their husbands, with love and obedience.

These scriptures I gave is for marriage it should not be taken lightly; you should make time for each other daily. Intimacy is not sex, but it is holding each other, and if it end up leading to making love, that should not, be an issue. If the wife wants to make love, it should not be a problem for the husband, and I am sure that he normally agrees to love making, with his wife.

It is a problem, with the wife, wanting to make love only went she wants to, because she wants to control the husband. Big problems are develop, if the husbands go outside of the marriage to be satisfy. Now, Pastor, why is that a problem when a man going outside of the marriage to be satisfied.

Well Brother Earnest, this is the problem you have went you go outside of the agreed union that was made before God, because you agreed not to leave or forsake your wife.

Pastor, it is hard to understand the female; she will be sexual if she is a prostitute or loss her man and is now looking for another man. For wives to say they are not in the mood to make love; when she is working the same job and doing the same things, that she was doing when she met this man. That is right Brother Earnest, but she can not control her job and plus she is making money. I believe that she feels that she is not getting enough money from the household account to do as she pleases.

Okay Brother Earnest, let me state this, there may be children now, and she may be thinking of their future; clothe, school; homework, friends, and neighborhood. Because, it is important to the husband and wife, too care for their children.

Pastor, I think we come up with things for women because we want too, and from the man point of view this give men their reason to see other women. The wife will put the husband on lock-down just because, she thinks she can and that's supposed to be okay.

But the though of men are, if you don't want to make love with me then there are many of other women out there that will.

Women need to understand, or there should be some other women telling these women that want to be married, that the mans sex drive is going to be greater then hers, dose she still want to get married.

Because if you can not perform in the bedroom, your husband will at some point find a women that will make love to him. Marriage is to give pleasure to one another, and not allow the other spouse to seek pleasure from some one else.

Divorce, can happen because one spouse dose not want to have sex any longer. What went wrong? That made that spouse not want to make love? Look Brother Earnest, all of that, that you stated is real: but, When Christ is in your life, and you apply God's Word to your life daily you will not have a reason of denying your spouse your body.

However, if God is in your life, then your mind is on the veracity of God Word to do according to the scripture. False, truths are in the mouth of many people just so they can get; what they are looking for and fright the other person for trying to get, what they want.

If you are going to fright your spouse over making love then it would have been better that you not married. Don't get married because that is what your friends are doing. But get married because you love and like this person and understand your responsibility as the male and female.

Adjustments are made so that you can make the marriage relationship better, but make sure there is an understanding of your responsibility, so that you both work well together. God made people, so that they can married and He place the organs for sex in your bodies. So the number of times a week, you make love, is not important, because He has place in us a feeling that will have us rest, as we did on the honeymoon, one night, just to pick-up from were we left off two night before.

Making love between husband and wife (male and female) two or more times per week will reduce heart attacks, stress, and depression according to a medical journal report. It also leads to strong communication and other playtime, with relaxation.

We tell ourselves that I am controlling the other spouse sexual activities and I will let him or her knows when we will do that again. I truly believe that, because we want to control this important activity, we are loosing our marriages because of that. Now if the husband wants to control the wife body and feel that it is necessary to violate his wife's body and "brow-beat" her with scripture.

What is the real problem here? Is it because she does not want to make love any longer or is she not truly in God's Word. Because the word said, dwell with your wife according to her knowledge of the Word of God. Therefore, the wife can or will not know how to take care of her husband sex drive, because she dose not know God's Word.

One thing for sure it is a job, to make changes daily to keep the marriage vows and scripture at the top of our list for doing the right thing. When we put God in our hearts and mine we stand a greater chance of improving our marital relationship.

We should understand that we have a sexual obligation (a promise), out of the love that we have for each other; we should enjoy each others body and spirit, where it should not have become a crisis, as we grow together in God's love to each other.

Looking at another person to have a sexual relationship will not get you more sex, only a headache; or a heartache, because your wife body is made the same as the other women that your looking at.

I guess, saints your going to need to prayer real hard for yourself and your spouse, and really study God's Word, in order that you remain faithful to your spouse even when she/he is not right with you. It may be a long time in your eyes, but just whole on anyhow, God will see you through this test in your life, and your faith will be the stronger.

We are always tested so why not this as a test; Satan will break down your marriage, if you have not learn of God, let the darts come your way follow God and prayer to Him. I know you feel that you need to make love and you love making love, this is not all mental, because God gave us the organs, He will give you, your spouse back sexually making the bedroom comfortable again.

God is the answer to all questions and will resolve every test if you trust Him, have faith in Him, and believe in Him. There is not a friend like Jesus, and you can call on Him any time, for anything, that's in your way, love God, to enjoy being married, so that He is in your marriage we lie to God and our spouse about many things.

Man hood and woman hood are not given because of an event of love making or child birth, but by the grace of God that has humble you to have His love, by your faith in him. And your knowledge of His Word, that will direct your path and the path of your future. Physical strength and money will not grant you the mercy and grace that you will need from God to do right to your fellow brother and sister, but you must surrender yourself and repent to God to receive His mercy that He has given to you.

So, why not let God direct us, to do the right thing for our marriage and ourselves. If you love, why lie, for God see and hear all that we do to ourselves and to each other. Marriage is between man, the husband and wife, the women, because it is right and it is very good, physically and spiritually, under heaven. Now brothers and sisters the scripture is; "Hebrews 13:4-Marriage is honorable and the bed is not broken."

If you remember the wedding vows, here they are, let me read than to you;

"Dearly beloved: We are gathers together here in the sight of God, and in the face of this company. To join together this Man and this Woman in holy matrimony, Which is commended of St. Paul to be honorable among all men; and therefore is not by any to be entered into unadvisedly, and in the fear of God.

Into this holy estate, these two persons present come now to be joined. If any man can show just cause why they may not lawfully be joined together, let him now Speak; or else hereafter forever hold his peace.

The minister shall say to the man:

Will you have this Woman to thy wedded wife, to live together after God's ordnance, in the holy estate of matrimony? Wilt thou love her, comfort her, honor, and keep her, in sickness and in health; and, forsaking all others, keep thee only unto her, so long as ye both shall Live?

The man shall answer, I will

Then shall the minister say to the woman:

Will you have this Man to thy wedded husband, to live together after God's ordnance, in the holy estate of matrimony? Wilt thou obey him and serve him, love, honor, and keep him, in sickness and in health; and, forsaking all others, keep thee only unto him, so long as ye both shall live?

The woman shall answer, I will:

The rings are given

The man repeats after the minister

As a pledge and a token of the vows between us made, with this ring I thee wed: In the name of the Father, and Of the Son, and of the Holy Ghost. Amen.

Woman repeats after the minister

As a pledge and a token of the vows between us made, with this ring I thee wed: In the name of the Father, and of the Son, and of the Holy Ghost. Amen.

Those, whom God hath joined together, let no man put asunder.

For as much as the man, and the woman, have consented together in holy wedlock, and have witnessed the same before God. And this company, and thereto have pledged their faith, each to the other, by giving and receiving a ring, and by joining their hands, I pronounce them Man and Wife together, in the name of the Father, and of the Son, and of the Holy Ghost. Amen. A Prayer."

If sick, other health issues, money issues, and that you agree to forsake all men/women, but your husband/wife. If you committed adultery you will be judge for this before, God if you touch someone that is not your spouse. You must repent before God, and ask God forgiveness; and go to your husband/wife and confess your sin to him/her and ask him/her forgiveness.

By doing this: God sees that you are sincere in your repentance: He will forgive you.

Your, husband/wife, may or may not forgive you.

Now, if your husband/wife is honest and is in Christ Jesus; let us read "Matthews 18:21-22 Then came Peter to him, and said, Lord, how often shall my brother sin against me, and I forgive him? Till seven times? Jesus said unto him, I say not unto thee, until seven times: but, until seventy times seven." he/she would know if they are in Christ Jesus. Because, he/she would know, that they, have not been treating you the way that the scripture said; that husbands and wives should only be a part for a short time.

This is big, if he/she is truly in Christ and understand the veracity of God's Word; than you would not need to be with another men/women. But, the husband/wife may not have been in Christ Jesus. Because, this has happen and the husband/wife will be upset and embarrass and he/she may file for a divorce or forgive you, if they are in Christ Jesus.

If any man/women that is going outside of their marriage, and put their marriage under, he/she is not in the spirit of Christ Jesus. If any men/woman push their spouse away that cause him/her to find another men/women for his/her satisfaction; he/she has sin against their spouse and God: and the husband/wife has also sin against God; for denying their spouse, their body.

Any men or a woman who denied their spouse intercourse, because of illness it is in your vows, otherwise it is a sin, and because you have control over the other one's bodies as it is record. In "I Corinthian 7:3-5 Let the husband render unto the wife due benevolence: and likewise also the wife unto the husband.

The wife have no power of her own body, but the husband: and likewise also the husband hath not power of his own body, but the wife. Defraud you not one the other, except it be with consent for a time, that ye may give yourselves to fasting and prayer; and come together again, that Satan tempt you not for your incontinency."

The scripture for marriage is a contract between God, the husband and the wife; and marriages should not be enter into lightly. The scriptures hold you to having sexual union when the other spouse wants their body, which belong to them.

If you are apart for fasting and praying them you must come back so that Satan (sin) dose not enter into the marriage union, so that no one will refuse to have intercourse. Every one of us will be judge on how we treated our spouse, selfish with money, selfish with making love; selfish with how the children are reared.

And spending too much time with other people, and not spending time with your spouse. We need to understand that we enter into a marriage that said, I will not allow anyone or anything to put this union under or to pull it down.

Now, Sister Walker and Sister Grace, are right as men and women of God you are going to have to study God's Word to know that it is true. In order that any touch on your hip or pull on your waste or rub on your chest should not give off, a signal, to reject your spouse for their advances.

Who, else is in that bed, and however long ago it has been, why are you confessing to be a follow of Christ; while in your bedroom, you have the spirit of Satan. God is the spirit of love. Understand, if, you are ill, or you had a loss of a love one or a great disruption, your spouse would be in prayer with you, and for being intimate (holding you) this is not sexual.

But, how long do we suffer the innocent spouse, with our pretense of love, have we been to God with our pain and have we left it with Him; so God can heal us. Our marriages are destroyed by our own hands; because of our hate of self, and do not care to remember that we have suffering our spouse unjustly.

Our love of God and our spouse: should be the thing that we keep in mind at all times, and not to have a nice thing, that we have grown to tolerate one another.

If our love of God was great and true them our love of our spouse is real, there are know hang up. No saying, no no, stalling, no games, all is for real, our love for and in Christ Jesus, and this would make our love to each other trues too God, and us.

If the honeymoon identify how you are going to make love, in the marriage, it would have been okay, if it, remained, that way after the honeymoon. The lovemaking should not have been cut off, because that is what he/she wants to do.

Now, I said a lot, but I needed to state, what I did, because of the scripture that I just read to you. Understanding, I think, this is the truth of every ones marriage; if it, was based on the honeymoon and some month after the honeymoon. Which, person, allow the problems to enter into the marital relationship; was it because of people at work, that you have talk about what's going on in your home, in your bedroom, issues with family and friends, even parents.

Your question, to yourself should be, why do I have a problem, or how come I know long make love, we are doing every thing that we can; but being loving and truthful. Because, if you desire to make love, to someone else, it truly said, that you do love, making love, just not with your spouse.

Why is this a question? Sister Black, yes, I know that I am not marred, but what is it that women go through after they are marred to not want to make love with their husband. Okay!

Okay! Pastor, can I try to help Sister Black, go right a head Sister William? Okay! Okay! It was like this. I didn't understand that I needed to have intercourse almost every night now. But it was our nature as women that came in and change my desire for having intercourse, and my attitude about having intercourse.

So I did not want to have sexual union, as much as my husband wanted me to. That happened to us women, not wanting to make love. My husband is a good man and I can not help him, in the state of mind that I am in. It is like, I don't know how it happened to me, that my mind and body just turned a corner, one day, and it removed my desire of sex.

Yes, my husband suffered, and I don't know how to explain this to him, because all the women of the world can not change this from happening to their bodies. I don't know if it's; because of age or just the mind of women change, and that slowed my desire for making love down: or I wanted more money or things for my love making.

And, I don't know how to turn the desire for intercourse back on, so my husband would know longer suffer, and think that I just don't want to be with him any longer. I was really upset when it appear that I could not think of making love, with my husband and I felt that other women knew that I was not able to be sexual, with my husband any more.

It appeared that all the other women are in his face to offer him sex, that's, what I was thinking; that I could not gave my husband: what is his, my body. So, I got my husband doing things, like doing work in the house, cooking, cleaning, helping with the children, going to the store and he never said, one cross word, but okay honey, what else, do you need.

I just wanted him to said, no, I am not doing any more, of that stuff, that's women work, so that I would argue with him, then I, would not have to make love, with him that night. In stead, I became upset; because I could not upset him, so I stopped him from getting any sex from me, because I am not there mentally to make love.

My husband went into a prayer mold, so I just stopped, no lovemaking. Until, he told me that Sunday to pull my panty up, I had put myself on a difference road and wanted to see if other men notice me. It was like Deacon William, saw through everything. I knew I needed to repent and Deacon William gave these scriptures to me, that the Pastor shared with us.

I realized that I lied to God and my husband, no one, could treat me the way Deacon William has, and now for the first time, I realized that I put our marriage under, because of my conduct, and attitude.

You see sisters, you want a good man, than you try to break him down, so that he will do what you want; because he is a man of God: God will break you down to obey and submit to your husband.

After studying all the scripture for months and got the theologian view I shouted and walked into the bedroom, naked, because I wanted Deacon William to see what is his. I said to Deacon William honey will you look at me, so he said, what's wrong, I said, nothing, will you hold me, he said, yes is there a problem.

I said, yes, I would like for you to forgive me, for the way that I have treated you for months. He said, Sister William I forgive you. As you have asked, then I said Kiss me. Sister William, are you all right. Yes, Pastor I am all right now. I told Deacon William, I prayed to God; for how I treated him, and I repented before God. And the Lord let me know that I had to go to Deacon William; and asked him to forgive me, and that I should not hold my body from my husband, because that is sinful.

I removed my lips from Deacon William lips and said I am so sorry, he said okay: Now what? Where do we go from here? I told him, I was in the spirit of Satan; even when I spent so much time in the church building, I was not in the spirit of God, with you my husband in our home and in our bedroom.

Ladies, I took my position as a follower of Christ, to obey my husband and to submit to my husband in everything. Just like the word said. It is good to have a new start on life, to start cleaning up your sinful ways. We need to start in our homes and once we've been, delivered to start in the neighborhood.

Pastor think you, sister and brother thank you, Deacon William thank you. Okay, saints is there anyone else, yes, Pastor, Sister Grace; now Sister William just ran off with this discussion, but I know that, that is a hard thing for us women to do for our husband, because we tell ourselves that this is my body.

But, if we truly search the scripture, Christ said that he loves the church; and men need to love their wives as they love themselves. The church (people) are doing all difference types of sins, but God still loves the church, he blesses the church, even if it is been good or bad.

We, do not want intercourse, with our husbands, but may be we want intercourse with a person at work, or some person in the church, or some person we just saw on the street. We have shifted our focus from love to lust, with some other man/woman, because we want to try someone else new.

Chapter 12

Christ And the Church

God made all men with the same organs, and He made all women with the same organs. The body of men are made the same, as is the body of women, are made the same, some parts may be pronounced more than others. But they are the same.

I know that the Pastor will be talking about divorce, because if we so call women in Christ; don't get our understanding of God's Word right, many of us may be heading for divorce. And we blame the other woman, when we are the other women, that may have created this problem for ourselves, and is now feeling that I don't need to understand God's Word, to correct anything that I may have done.

We, the wife, are just as much the blame, for the divorce, if it happens, if your husband felt he needed to go outside of the marriage just to be satisfy. He has committed the act of adultery; because of the wife hard position in regard to her body. Because of the lack of biblical knowledge, she has become ignorance to the Word of God.

The man is ignorance to God's Word; if he did not apply the word to his life, directing him from making selfish decision. Thank you, Pastor Johnson for letting us women speak the truth about, God's Word and apply His Word to our lives.

As your Pastor, wait just one minute Pastor, okay Sisters Johnson, go right ahead. I have sat and listen to the sisters and brothers indicate the sexual problems in their household. But, it just didn't stop there, with the deacons or other officers of the church including the other members. The Pastor had it hard as well, and I, Sister Johnson had to learn through the scriptures to follow Christ; as his wife, to make myself available to my husband, the Pastor, without having an attitude.

You see, Christ is real, and the problems in the home are too, with the wife and the husband, the bedroom; intimacy/love making is the biggest problem in every marriage: I truly believe that. And you know ladies we created this problem, in our bedroom from the beginning of our marriage.

And, we as women, really do not think that our husband, are worth us all the time. Because, we tell ourselves that we are special and my needs come before his needs. But if your husband is a true man of God, you must take care of his needs, too have your needs fulfilled.

And, if your husband is not a man of God, you still must take care of his needs and keep him in prayer, that God will save him from, himself. Yes, you know why, we are getting a divorce, so don't said, I did not see it coming; when you have not wanted to make love in the past three to six months or a year or two.

Stop, lying to yourselves, about your marital relationship; you know that you are having problems, because you stop making love. Your husband, will never stop making love and every women knows that, so stop the lies, and seek God for your direction. Thank you Pastor.

Thank you everyone, okay, Pastor thank you, Sister Grace, Sister Walker, Sister William, and Sister Johnson, okay, Brother Brown, divorce, why Pastor?

There are many reason for divorce, spouse in adultery, spouse spend to much money, spouse abuse, spouse addict to drug, spouse is an alcoholic, spouse may be over weight, or the spouse may have started an affair with someone that is gray or an lesbian.

Spouse may be a gambler, spouse may not be given the other spouse quality time, spouse may want to make love every four to six months, and the spouse may be spending too much time in the church. These are a few of the reason including untruthfulness, and no God; no love. Men have the most important position in the family, because he is head of the household.

Therefore, the husband, better make very sure, that he is in Christ Jesus; not only keep himself together; but to may sure that he can endure the challenges that would come into his life. God will test this man, to see if he is able to stand, difficult time even before he gets married. God will allow this man to go through something that will make him wonder, what is going on, with my trust, in God.

You see; the test that God put you through; will better help you to understand your godly character; on how you will think? What God would do in this saturation? So, little do we know as men, that God prepares' us for marriage. Because, in your marriage you will have many challenges, so if your faith is in God and you believe in Him, God will see you through.

Then, as things get out of control, in your marriage and in your home with your children; you will remember to keep your prayer unto God.

As men we must understand that the man was made in the image of God. Remember God said, in;

"Genesis 1:26-27 And God said, Let us make man in our image, after our likeness: and let them have dominion over the fish of the sea, and over the fowl of the air, and over the cattle, and all the earth, and over every creeping thing that creep upon the earth. So God created man in his own image, in the image of God created he him; male and female created he them."

We have made, some wrong choices, in the type of occupation, for ourselves, (gangs, crime, and occupations that did not allow us to grow) it has cause many problems, with our attitudes and other issues. We must understand God's Word; to advance in this world, and to understand how we can move through the politic; to accomplish what we need to, in this world through Christ Jesus.

If we as men, are truly in Christ Jesus, and are applying His Word, than there will not be a problem for us to stop those activity that are not of God. If we have backslide into doing worldly things; than we should turn to God to get us out of that situation and back on track. Now, God created the women for the man, and not the man for the women.

It is very important that husbands and wives be in a relationship, with God for their peace of mind and for the safety and sanity of their marriage. There is not a scripture about domestic violence in the bible, but the scripture tells us to love our wives as Christ love the church.

We are to love our wife as we love ourselves, for no man will hurt his self or beat or abuse himself, so why, abuse your wife; which God have given unto you, for protection, caring, loving, kindness and she has had children for you. For if you do this to your wife you are in sin and not in a relationship with Jesus Christ. We must always be in prayer daily, as we begin our day and throughout the day we should always be in prayer about all things.

Okay here is what the bible said; Ephesians "5:20-33 Giving thanks always for all things unto God and the Father in the name of our Lord Jesus Christ; Submitting yourselves one to another in the fear of God. Wives, submit yourselves unto your own husbands, as unto the Lord. For the husband is the head of the wife, even as Christ is the head of the church: and he is the Savior of the body.

Therefore as the church is subject unto Christ, so let the wives be to their own husbands in everything. Husband, love your wives, even as Christ also loved the church, and gave himself for it; That he might sanctify and cleanse it with the washing of water by the word,

That he might present it to himself a glorious church, not having spot, or wrinkle, or any such thing; but that it should be holy and without blemish. So ought men to love their wives as their own bodies. He that love his wife love himself. For no man ever yet hated his own flesh; but nourish and cherish it, even as the Lord the church: For we are members of his body, of his flesh, and of his bones.

For this cause shall a man leave his father and mother and shall be joined unto his wife, and they two shall be one flesh. This is a great mystery: but I speak concerning Christ and the church. Nevertheless let every one of you in particular so love his wife even as himself; and the wife see that she reverence her husband."

Colossians "3; If you then be risen with Christ, seek those things which are above, where Christ sit on the right hand of God. Set your affection on things above, not on things on the earth. For you are dead, and your life is hid with Christ in God. When Christ, who is our life, shall appear, then shall you also appear with him in glory.

Mortify therefore your members which are upon the earth; fornication, uncleanness, inordinate affection, evil concupiscence, and covetousness, which is idolatry: For which things sake the wrath of God come on the children of disobedience: In the which you also walked some time, when you lived in them. But now you also put off all these; anger, wrath, malice, blasphemy, filthy communication out of your mouth.

Lie not one to another, seeing that you have put off the old man with his deeds; And have put on the new man, which is renewed in knowledge after the image of him that created him: Where there is neither Greek nor Jew, circumcision nor uncircumcision,

Barbaraian, Scythian, bond nor free: but Christ is all, and in all.

Put on therefore, as the elect of God, holy and beloved, bowels of mercies, kindness, humbleness of mind, meekness, long suffering; Forbearing one another, and forgiving one another, if any man have a quarrel against any: even as Christ forgave you, so also do you. And above all these things put on charity, which is the bond of perfection.

And let the peace of God rule in your hearts; called in one body; and be yet thankful. Let the word of Christ dwell in you richly in all wisdom; teaching and admonishing one another in psalms and hymns and spiritual songs, singing with grace in your hearts to the Lord. And whatsoever you do in word or deed, do all in the name of the Lord Jesus, giving thanks to God and the Father by him.

Wives, submit yourselves unto your own husbands, as it is fit in the Lord. Husbands, love your wives, and be not bitter against them. Children obey your parents in all things: for this is well pleasing unto the Lord. Fathers, provoke not your children to anger, lest they be discouraged.

Servants, obey in all things your masters according to the flesh; not with eye-service, as men please; but in singleness of heart, fearing God: And whatsoever you do, do it heartily, as to the Lord, and not unto men; knowing that of the Lord; you shall receive the reward of the inheritance: for you serve the Lord Christ. But he that do wrong shall receive for the wrong, which he have done: and there is no respect of person."

I Thessalonians "3; Wherefore when we could no longer forbear, we though it good to be left at Athens alone; And sent Ti-moth-e-us, our brother, and minister of God, and our fellow-laborer in the gospel of Christ, to establish you, and to comfort you concerning your faith: That no man should be moved by these afflictions: for yourselves know that we are appointed thereunto.

For verily, when we were with you, we told you before that we should suffer tribulation; even as it came to pass, and you know. For this cause, when I could no longer forbear, I sent to know your faith, lest by some means the tempter have tempted you, and our labor be in vain. But now when Ti-moth-e-us came from you unto us, and brought us good tidings of your faith an charity, and that you have good remembrance of us always, desiring greatly to see us, as we also to see you:

Therefore, brethren, we were comforted over you in all of our affliction and distress by your faith: For now we live, if you stand fast in the Lord. For what thanks can we render to God again for you, for all the joy wherewith we joy for your sakes before our God; Night and day praying exceedingly that we might see your face, and might perfect that which is lacking in your faith?

Now God himself and our Father, and our Lord Jesus Christ, direct our way unto you. And the Lord made you to increase and abound in love one toward another, and toward all men, even as we do toward you: To the end he may stable your hearts not blame able in holiness before God, even our Father, at the coming of our Lord Jesus Christ with all his saints."

The spiritual law should help us to obey the earthly laws, and our faith in God; makes God please with us. If the man that you are married to; abuse you, get away to safety, and let the authority know of your situation with your husband or wife. Please, know that if, he/she puts their hands on you once, they would likely do it again.

Call the people that can put them in line, the police. You should not be, in fear from the one person, on this earth that they said; that they are in love with you. It made be an embarrassment to you; because of the love that you have for them; and how much they said; that they loved you. Call family and friends to let them know that this incident has taken place. You need to be pro-activist to this type of situation; it can be deadly, if not address.

"Genesis 2:18,21-25 And the Lord God said, It is not good that the man should be alone; I will make him an help meet for him.

And the Lord God caused a deep sleep to fall upon Adam, and he slept: and he took one of his ribs, and closed up the flesh instead thereof; And the rib, which the Lord God had taken from man, made he a woman, and brought her unto the man.

And Adam said, This is now bone of my bones, and flesh of my flesh: she shall be called Woman, because she was taken out of Man. Therefore shall a man leave his father and his mother, and shall cleave unto his wife: and they shall be one flesh. And they were both naked, the man and his wife, and were not ashamed."

If we have remained on course, with God and His Word: than we should understand and realize that when things; becomes difficult and it is not going the way that we would like it to go. Then we know that we must go to God in prayer. We had though for a long period of time, that women where more godly than men were; because more women are in the church building, than men.

But overtime most men have found, that most women and men are not more godly; than the other. They are just in the church to get the man/woman; that is in the image of godliness, so that man/woman would speak to them and treat them with love and respect.

Now, Pastor, is that the reason, why women are in hopes that the man will asked them to married him. Well Brother Right; that may be the case with some women, but I do not believe that is the case with all women. But, before the man can claim a woman: he must first know how to defend and subdue things in his life; as stated by God.

Genesis 1:28" And God blessed them, and God said unto them, be fruitful, and multiply, and replenish the earth, and subdue it: and have dominion over the fish of the sea, and over the fowl of the air, and over every living thing that move upon the earth."

The women need a man that can endure all things; at any time and any were in his life. When that man takes a wife he should protect her, and provide for her until he dies.

The man is in the image of God and he is ruler over the women, not in dictatorship; but in making decision that should make the home a safer and better place. This is what the scripture said.

"Genesis 3:16-Unto the woman he said, I will greatly multiply your sorrow and your conception; in sorrow you shall bring forth children; and your desire shall be to your husband, and he shall rule over you."

God places this on Eve because she did not listen to God and her husband about the trees in the center of the garden. But, the rule was over turn with God's Word; it return the husband and wife back to the beginning as it was with Adam and Eve.

Mary gave birth to Jesus, which lifted the disobedience of Eve. Therefore the husband must treat their wife just like Christ treat the church. Christ said, I would not leave you or forsake you (the church).

Men Christ suffered and died for us; men you must bear some burdens with your wives.

Ephesians "5:25-27 Husbands, love your wives, even as Christ also loved the church, and gave himself for it; That he might sanctify and cleanse it with the washing of water by the word, That he might present it to himself a glorious church, not having spot, or wrinkle, or any such thing; but that it should be holy and without blemish."

Chapter 13

Divorce

Okay, Pastor, how dose divorce play into the marriage at this point? Brother Mart, marriage is sacred; like Christ and the church, so are man and wife. Christ died for us the church and man hold to his wife; because she is the spirit of the man and she will carry life in her for the man. The church and the women are delicate in nature and must be taken care of, for the church is not a head of Christ and the wife is not a head of the husband.

For the life, that the wife will carry, will be future followers of Christ; so it is very important that the man in Christ: married the woman in Christ so that their children will learn to worship Christ; to follow Christ. Her fountain should only be for the husband to drink from and no others.

And, the husband should know, that the children are taught by him and the wife; being a father and they are from the same women. For the bond is establish on their wedding night, by the blood meaning a sacrifice from the wife to the husband. That, the husband on that night, establish ownership of the wife body, and the wife establish ownership of the husband body; their covenant or bond, bonded them; that night one to another.

That the husband; now know of his wife, and the wife; now know of her husband, and know one else: should know of what they know; about each other, but themselves. Brother Mart: when we think of divorce wemust understand that it is truly a tearing of the covenant; that has been established between husband and wife.

If you remember the wedding vows, here they are "

Dearly beloved: We are gather; together here in the sight of God, and in the face of this company. To join together this Man and this Woman in holy matrimony, which is commended of St. Paul to be honorable among all men; and therefore is not by any to be entered into unadvisedly, and in the fear of God.

Into this holy estate, these two persons present come now to be joined. If any man can show just cause why they may not lawfully be joined together, let him now speak, or else hereafter forever hold his peace.

The minister shall say to the man:

Will you have this Woman to thy wedded wife, to live together after God's ordnance, in the holy estate of matrimony? Wilt thou love her, comfort her, honor, and keep her, in sickness and in health; and, forsaking all others, keep thee only unto her, so long as yea both shall live?

The man shall answer, I will

Then shall the minister say to the woman:

Will you have this Man to thy wedded husband, to live together after God's ordnance, in the holy estate of matrimony? Wilt thou obey him and serve him, love, honor, and keep him, in sickness and in health; and, forsaking all others, keep thee only unto him, so long as ye both shall live?

The woman shall answer, I will:

The rings are given

The man repeats after the minister

As a pledge (as a promise) and in token (as a keepsake) of the vows between us made, with this ring I thee wed:

In the name, of the Father; and of the Son; and of the Holy Ghost. Amen.

The woman repeats after the minister

As a pledge (as a promise) and in token (as a keepsake) of the vows between us made, with this ring I thee wed: In the name of the Father, and of the Son, and of the Holy Ghost. Amen.

Those, whom God hath joined together, let no man put asunder.

For as much as the man, and the woman, have consented together in holy wedlock, and have witnessed the same before God and this company. And thereto have pledged their faith, each to the other, by giving and receiving a ring, and by joining their hands, I pronounce them Husband and Wife together, in the name of the Father, and of the Son, and of the Holy Ghost. Amen.

A Prayer."

Because, Christ's covenant was made between Him and the church, as stated in Hebrews 13:5 "Let your conversation be without covetousness; and be content with such things as ye have: for he hath said, I will never leave thee, nor forsake thee."

Brother Pastor, yes, Sister Black, I want to know; am I anew now: because I have repented for my sins and turn my life over to God?

Yes, Sister Black, now you must spend your time serving God; having faith in God and believing in God.

Because you took off the old person and have now come to Christ to be a sinner save by grace. This means that; your out-look on life is difference and your spirit about things, should be difference. You should be looking at the good in people and just not focus on their negative.

You have a new attitude, a loving attitude for people, a forgiving attitude, and a caring attitude for people. Everything about you has become anew, because you are in Christ Jesus. Is my body healed, if your mind is healed, God will heal your body from how it was used before in sin.

So, what type of man do I think would want to married me, after everything I have done in my life. Look Sister Black; if what you tell your husband, to be, is going to help him, better understand you as a person than tell him. If it is not going to help right than, thin wait; but tell him before you get married, because it will come up later.

And it may be out of control, doing the time that it will happen. Listen saints how important is marriage to you. So, what you say, and what you do, will have some type of a impact on your marriage and these things could lead you to divorce.

Sister Johnson, my wife got up and said, what she had to do, to become a committed saint to God, and to me; but there were things that I knew; I had to do also. I asked God; why did he have me married Sister Johnson; if she was not in the word and committed, as I. The Lord let me know that; because I was trying to serve Him, then men need to be like Christ; bearing his wife pain, as Christ bear the pain for the church. If you are in God, more than your spouse than you must bear the pain, and through your worship of God; in His time, God will mode the other spouse.

Look at I Corinthians 7:11-16 "But and if she depart, let her remain unmarried, or be reconciled to her husband: and let not the husband put away his wife. But to the rest speak I, not the Lord: If any brother have a wife that believe not, and she will be pleased to dwell with him, let him not put her away. And the woman which have an husband that believe not, and if he were pleased to dwell with her, let her not leave him.

For the unbelieving husband; is sanctified by the wife, and the unbelieving wife; is sanctified by the husband: else were your children unclean; but now are they holy. But if the unbelieving depart, let him depart. A brother or a sister is not under bondage in such cases: but God has called us to peace.

For what know you, O wife, whether you shall save your husband? Or how do you know, O man, whether you shall save your wife?"

Teaching about Divorce-St. Matthew 19:1-12 "And it came to pass, that when Jesus had finished these sayings, he departed from Galilee, and came into the coasts of Judea beyond Jordan; And great multitudes followed him; and he healed them there.

The Pharisees also came unto him, tempting him, and saying unto him, Is it lawful for a man to put away his wife for every cause?

And he answered and said unto them, Have you not read, that he which made them at the beginning made them male and female, And said, For this cause shall a man leave father and mother, and shall cleave to his wife: and they twin shall be one flesh? Wherefore they are no more twin, but one flesh. What therefore God has joined together let not man put asunder.

They say unto him, Why did Moses then command to give a writing of divorce, and to put her away? He said unto them, Moses because of the hardness of your hearts suffered you to put away your wives: but from the beginning it was not so.

And I say unto you, Whosoever shall put away his wife, except it be for fornication, and shall marry another, commit adultery: and who so married her which is put away do commit adultery.

His disciples say unto him, If the case of the man be so with his wife, it is not good to marry. But he said unto them; All men cannot receive this saying, save they to whom it is given. For there are some eunuchs, which were so born from their mother's womb: and there are some eunuchs, which were made eunuchs of men: and there be eunuchs, which have made themselves eunuchs for the kingdom of heaven's sake. He that is able to receive it, let him receive it."

It was not easy, my wife wanted everything done her way and that was that. And because of that type of attitude it overflowed to the bedroom. I had to make sure that I understood God Word for myself. Than I went into prayer for my wife, myself and the family: But she would say, you better be praying for yourself, because I know God.

It was one day our youngest daughter said to her mother are you angry with daddy. My wife said no baby, so she said, then why are you talking to daddy like you talk to us children. Sister Johnson looked up at me and realize that the children heard her tone with me and her attitude was not of God, who teach love.

So, Sister Johnson got up and went to the bedroom and was walking and praying. When she came back to the family room Sister Johnson asked me about some scriptures. And Sister Johnson kept studying the word to understand what God really meant about love and how these scriptures showed her the meaning of love.

"I Corinthians 13:1-13 Though I speak with the tongues of men and of angels, and have not charity, I am become as sounding brass, or a tinkling cymbal.

And though I have the gift of prophecy, and understand all mysteries, and all knowledge; and though I have all faith, so that I could remove mountains, and have not charity, I am nothing. And though I bestow all my goods to feed the poor, and though I give my body to be burned, and have not charity, it profit me nothing.

Charity suffer long, and is kind; charity envy not; charity vaunt not itself, is not puffed up, Do this not behave itself unseemly, seek not her own, is not easily provoked, think no evil; Rejoice in the truth; Bear all things, believe all things, hope all things, endure all things.

Charity never fail: but whether there be prophecies, they shall fail; whether there be tongues, they shall cease; whether there be knowledge, it shall vanish away. For we know in part, and we prophesy in part. But when that which is perfect is come, then that which is in part shall be done away.

When I was a child, I spoke as a child, I understood as a child, I thought as a child: but when I became a man, I put away childish things. For now we see through a glass, darkly; but then face to face: now I know in part; but then shall I know even as also I am known. And now abide faith, hope, charity, these three; but the greatest of these is charity."

The out come is what you heard Sister Johnson shared with everyone early. God's Word is true and divorce only happen when there is no God in your life. Having God in your life; will help you depend on God, as your problems surface.

Here are some more scriptures; Number 30: 7-12 7) "And her husband heard it, and held his peace at her in the day that he heard it; then her vows shall stand, and her bonds where with she bound her soul shall stand.

But if her husband disallowed her on the day that he heard it; then he shall make her vow which she vowed, and that which she uttered with her lips, where with she bound her soul, of none effect: and the Lord shall forgive her. But every vow of a widow, and of her that is divorced, where with they have bound their souls, shall stand against her. And if she vowed in her husband's house, or bound her soul by a bond with an oath;

And her husband heard it, and held his peace at her, and disallowed her not: then all her vows shall stand, and every bond wherewith she bound her soul shall stand. But if her husband has utterly made them void on the day he heard them; then whatsoever proceeded out of her lips concerning her vows, or concerning the bond of her soul, shall not stand: her husband has made them void; and the Lord shall forgive her."

Now Pastor, Sister little; but just one-minute Sister little: I just want to explain these verses, okay, Pastor.

In these verses of Numbers we are discussing divorce, and in these times the husband if silence, when the wife wanted a divorce, she would be granted the divorce. If the husband said no or void what she said, she would not receive the divorce.

If she wanted to leave her father house and he was silence then she can go, if the father void her request then she could not leave.

The weight would be on the father or the husband if a daughter or a wife wanted to leave. To be honest today we have legal papers drawing up for a divorce and husband and wife must both sign to process the divorce.

Now about the father in today world when daughter feel that they are physically, emotional and financially able to support themselves they want to be able get their own place. Okay, Sister Little go right ahead with: what you were going to say. Thank you Pastor; last week in bible class and to night bible class Sister Walker and Sister Grace, they where jumping for joy, because they are not a shame of doing the right thing by their husband; but I disagree with what they're saying, about what you must do.

I read my bible and I don't think God will have me give my husband; what belong to my husband. Did I say that right, Wait! Wait! Pastor, where is that scripture that is addressing control of one another. Sister little, that scripture is in I Corinthian the seventh chapter and starting at verse 4 "The wife has not power of her own body, but the husband: and likewise also the husband has not power of his own body, but the wife." Yes, that's the one Pastor, so I must do what Pastor?

Well Sister Little, the first thing that you must do is go unto God; by repentance to Him for your sins. Asking God to forgive you and study God's Word and believe in the Word, and have faith in the Word by applying the Word by your faith and apply it to your daily life.

But Pastor, I had done all the praying, and studies for months; before it got into my spirit to truly love the Lord. Them I was able to truly love my husband, not push him away, or said no, or start an argument; just so I did not had to have intercourse with my husband.

This is a sin, because, if you told untruthful things to have control over your own body and not your husband body, this is not godly and you are not in the spirit of God, because God is love. Oh, I see, Pastor so I need to asked my husband to forgive me and repent to God, to receive my forgiveness from him.

Yes Sister Little, and if we all did this, how beautiful, our life and marriage would be; because of someone that we are in love with, we would want to please them, and not hurt him or her. God loves us; so he provides for us and helps us to draw closer to Him.

Therefore the more that you are in love with your spouse the closer you become and the bedroom is not a prison, but a bride chamber (honeymoon). Now Sisters Little are you all right with, what I just explain to you, yes Pastor.

I know Brother Little you're on top of this: okay Brother little, do you have any question; not really, Pastor, I just wanted to state, that I have tried to tell Sister Little for years about the scriptures.

And, she would tell me; you need to read them, because you must have the devil in you, that all that's on your mind, making love. I told her that she is mind and the bible said that; I have control over her and she have control over me. She will just said, I have control over you, and I am controlling this over here from you.

Okay, let us turn to:

St. Matthew 5:31-32 "It have been said, whosoever shall put away his wife, let him give her a writing of divorce. But I say unto you: That whosoever shall put away his wife, saving for the cause of fornication, cause her to commit adultery: and whosoever shall marry her that is divorced commit adultery."

The bloodline of the husband should make them his children and that his wife did not have intercourse outside of the marriage, with someone else because that is adultery, with a other person.

Okay, our next scripture, Deuteronomy 24:1-4 "When a man has taken a wife, and married her, and it come to pass that she find no favor in his eyes, because he has found some uncleanness in her. Then let him write her a bill of divorce, and give it in her hand, and send her out of his house.

And when she is departed out of his house, she may go and be another man's wife. And if the latter husband hate her, and write her a bill of divorce,

and give it in her hand, and send her out of his house; or if the latter husband die, which took her to be his wife;

Her former husband, which sent her away, may not take her again to be his wife, after that she is defiled; for that is abomination before the Lord: and you shall not cause the land to sin, which the Lord your God give you for an inheritance."

For unfaithfulness the reason the husbands, were allowed to divorce their wives and put them out.

The land if the husbands die was left within the tribe to share. But the husband share would go to the wife if they were still married.

Look at I Corinthians 7:10-16 "And unto the married I command, yet not I, but the Lord, Let not the wife depart from her husband: But and if she depart, let her remain unmarried, or be reconciled to her husband: and let not the husband put away his wife. But to the rest speak I, not the Lord: If any brother has a wife that believe not, and she will be pleased to dwell with him, let him not put her away. And the woman, which have a husband that believe not, and if he be pleased to dwell with her, let her not leave him.

For the unbelieving, husband is sanctified by the wife, and the unbelieving, wife is sanctified by the husband: else were your children unclean; but now are they holy. But if the unbelieving depart, let him depart. A brother or a sister is not under bondage in such cases: but God has called us to peace.

For what know you, O wife, whether you shall save your husband? Or how do you know you, O man, whether you shall save your wife?"

Less turn to Isaish 50: 1-3 "Thus say the Lord, Where is the bill of your mother's divorce, whom I have put away? Or which of my creditors is it to whom I have sold you? Behold, for your iniquities have you sold yourselves, and for your transgressions is your mother put away.

Wherefore, when I came, was there no man? When I called, was there none to answer? Is my hand shortened at all, that it cannot redeem? Or have I no power to deliver? Behold, at my rebuke I dry up the sea, I make the rivers a wilderness: their fish stink, because there is no water, and die for thirst. I clothe the heavens with blackness, and I make sackcloth their covering."

God wanted Israiel to repent for their sin and to have some compassion for what they have allow married men to do to their wives. They divorce them for unfaithfulness and the Jews priest did not use this as an example to this problem. So, God allow Israiel to be in bonded by Babylonies and sold as slaves to their enemies. So here we are at this scripture.

"St. Matthew 19:4-9 And he answered and said unto them, have you not read, that he which made them at the beginning made them male and female. And said: For this cause shall a man leave father and mother, and shall cleave to his wife: and they twin shall be one flesh?

Wherefore they are no more twin, but one flesh. What therefore God has joined together, let not man put asunder. They say unto him, why did Moses then command to give a writing of divorce, and to put her away? He said unto them, Moses because of the hardness of your hearts suffered you to put away your wives: but from the beginning it was not so. And I say unto you, Whosoever shall put away his wife, except it be for fornication, and shall marry another, commit adultery: and who so married her which is put away you commit adultery."

St. Mark 10:2-12 "And the Pharisees came to him, and asked him, Is it lawful for a man to put away his wife? tempting him.

And he answered and said unto them. What did Moses command you? And they said Moses suffered to writer a bill of divorce, and to put her away. And Jesus answered and said unto them, For the hardness of your heart he wrote you this precept.

But from the beginning of the creation God made them male and female. For this cause shall a man leave his father and mother, and cleave to his wife;

And they twin shall be one flesh; so then they are no more twin, but one flesh.

What therefore God has joined together let not man put asunder. And in the house his disciples asked him again of the same matter. And he said unto them, whosoever shall put away his wife, and marry another, commit adultery against her.

And if a women shall put away her husband, and be married to another, she commit adultery."

We must be careful entering into marriage because of the two purposes of the marriage God command. To be fruitful and multiply and the man being in the image of Christ and the woman to represent the church. Marriage is an, until death do we part commitment, good or hard times, you are in it for the duration of your married life.

There should never be a reason that adultery should enter into the marriage, if the, husband/wife are truly in Christ Jesus. When adultery does enter the marriage the spouse that brought it into the marriage is going to be punish by God and an earth punishment of divorce.

If the spouse did not make themselves available to their spouse they to will be punish by God; because your body is his and his is yours, and the other part will be done through divorce.

No one will escape God's wrath, lies about how you feel, but you say, that you are in love and the one that committed the sin for not holding on and praying to God for strength, and praying for your spouse for their love, kindness and understanding.

It is very importance to study the scriptures to know; what is needed in your walk with Christ to improve your life with your loved ones. We are going to go further with husband and wife in next week bible classes. Brother Little, would you prayer for us as we end tonight class. "Oh, holy and all mighty God, we think you for this class tonight, thank you for showing my wife the understanding of your word that it is about obedience, submission and service to God.

That if we receive God's love and keep it in our minds that we will be able to love one another and love our spouse and not keep them from us. As we go now we are asking for your protection to be with us at all times. In your son Jesus name. Amen! Amen! Amen!"

Okay, thank you for that prayer, Brother Little. We will see everyone at church Sunday and bible class, good night. As I walked to the car Jerry, Pauline, Michael and Franklin; where on their way from their bible class, Paul was close behind.

Hi, guys, hello, how was class tonight, it was good. I would have loved it; if your father were in our class tonight it was another great discussion on marriage and divorce. The Pastor said; that we need to know God and be true to God and repent unto God, for every sin.

Yea, mother that's, what dad said, in our class. He also said that it is a commitment for life, marriage is, and everything doses not always go your way. Dad said, that you must learn of the person you love through God's love; for our commitment to Christ.

For there are times that you don't understand her and she don't understand you. God is the glue, that will hold your marriage together when things are good and when times are challenging in the relationship. If we study God's Words and allow the Words to enter our mind, process it, store it and rely on it, and have faith and believe it.

Then you are starting to move in the right direction for your life. When you are doing this you are preparing yourself for grace to come your way. I am slowly starting to understand; what God wants from us. Well were home, everyone knows what they must do when we get in the house.

Okay dad, Paul I will tell you about Sister Little once we are in our bedroom. Okay children good night Jerry, Pauline, Michael, and Franklin; gave your mother a kiss and Pauline kiss your dad, you boys give dad a hug. Paul, Sister Little said, she disagree with what Sister Walker and I said; on last week and something that was stated tonight.

Then she said, I don't think God will have me give my husband what belongs to him. Then she asked the Pastor for the scripture. Paul; I am glad that you did not give up on me our first couple of years. But I know now more than ever; how God lives in us and how the Lord open my eyes and mind to study and understand; His Word to have us, have a blessed marriage and four beautiful children.

Paul I never wanted to hold my body from you, because when that happens other sin comes in that would lead to negative discussion about why I said no, when it is not the true about my feeling for you.

If after what you go through on your job and being with the children and with me. And when you touch my Hip; I have prepared my mind and body for the bride chamber by putting everything out of my spirit, and getting God's loving spirit, with you and in you arms, Paul. Every day through prayer and Christ love for me to be always ready for you.

It has not always been easy for me to be focus on you with all the many things that are on my mind. But, I remember, with all the things, I had to do; when we first got married: I made it my place to think about you, every minute of the day.

So, I really do not have any good reason why I don't think either of you daily; because I love God and I love you, Paul. I believe I know what it is? It is because I am comfortable, and I do not think of you like I did before; and I should not do that: because life is short and we should enjoy every minute of being happy in the Lord and with each other.

I really understood God's Word, because I should make it my passion to do God's will according to the scripture. And spend my life doing that and apply the scriptures to how I should be treating you and the children.

Now, Paul if you love me enough to want me, I know that I love you enough to want you. I never made up, any excuses when we, got married, so why did I make up excuses later. I think because, I wanted to be look at for my brains and not my body, just don't touch the body. We did have the children, a home, and a car and blessed with good jobs; so why did we need to make love as often as we did? I understood early in our marriage; about making love, because we wanted children.

I know I put things together, pleasure from love making, and enjoying having sex. But, I though that you would only want to make love after the children; when I wanted to make love; boy was I really wrong.

I never thought about how much you mint to me, and how much I mint to you. God's Word pulled me out of the sea of darkness; to stop me from telling you the untrue at all time, and at bedtime.

Chapter 14

A Forgiving Spirit of Others

I let everything pull me down and I expected you to pick my spirit up; and I blame you when my spirit was still down.

When the true of the manner was that I needed to go to God and asked Him; to forgive me and asked you to forgive me for how I was unfaithful and untruthful to you my husband. So after saying all of that Paul come to me just like this, it's our honeymoon.

Morning was here and the house was buzzing with the noise from the children, good morning everyone, good morning daddy and mother. We ate breakfast, and began going out the door; our parents to work and we were off to school.

The week appeared to be moving very quickly; before I knew it, it was Friday. And Beth and I wanted to go to the movies, because Susan had called Beth and told her, about this movie.

Why didn't you ask Jerry to call John to see if he and Jane would like to joint us? Beth called Jerry: Hell-o, hi Jerry, this is Beth, Susan called me and asked if you wanted to take in a moves. Well Beth; what is the movies about?

Women beating up on guys; hey, Jerry that's not nice! I am just playing Beth. So, will you call John, okay Beth, so what time did you say the movies started, at 7:00 P.M. Jerry. Okay I'll pick you up at 6:00 P.M., okay Beth. I'll see you than Jerry okay, by Beth.

You know Beth everything was really nice this evening; I hope bad boy Bob enjoyed everything. Bob and Susan appeared to be okay, but

Susan and Bob made sure that no one said anything out of the way about this movie.

When the movie was over Jane, Susan, and Bob went with John. And Beth and I drove in the opposite direction toward home. It was nice seeing everyone again, because it has been about a mouth since that last time we all went out together.

Yes, you're right Jerry, look Beth; what Jerry? It's a shooting star, oh yea it is; Why don't we stop Jerry? Okay, let me pull the car over off the road and onto the emergency lane; kiss me Jerry.

What's wrong! Just kiss me? Let me unfastened my seat belt, there. I just need to come over to you Beth. Okay Beth your pulling me closer to you. It was a kiss of passion and it went on for about five minutes than they pulled away from each other, with a look of should we continue kissing and go further.

A, Beth I want to, but that would not be a good ideal for either of us. Jerry I know your right, but I just; a tip on the car window, its the police, Oh hi office, is everything all right, just move along you can not stray in the emergency lane forever.

All right officer I'll just started the car and pulled off as the office was on his way back to his car. Wow, that was close, Beth I am glade we stopped kissing, before he pulled up. Yea, me to; what's wrong Beth?

What's wrong Jerry; I wanted you can't you see that, yes Beth I know that, and I want you but if we are going to be right before God. Then we must do the right things, Beth it only takes one time, than your pregnant, and there goes college for both of us.

But Jerry, we would have a baby, Beth we don't have a job to support ourselves never mind a baby. You're right Jerry, I wish our four years of college was already over, and we got married. My father already told me that a family is expensive and you need a good job to take care of your wife and then the cost of bring a children in the union is expenses.

We turn the corner, Beth what are you doing? I just want to hold your hand until we reached my house. I'll walk you to the door Beth. We got out of the car and I walked Beth to the front door; I hugged her then give her a short soft kiss on her lips.

Beth opened the door and went inside the house; as I walked back to my car. I started it, driving a few blocks to my house. Everyone was in the bed when I arrived home from the movies. So I put the car in the garage and went into the house.

When I reached the top of the stairs I walked down to my room; dad got out of his bed and ask, is everything all right. Sure dad; I will talk to you in the morning. Good night dad, good night Jerry.

It is so great to have a boy friend like Jerry, Beth said. And now I can think about this kiss to night as I lie in my bed, wanting to know how it would have been to have sex with Jerry. Jerry is right we must finish college first, then get married. Oh Man; let me get moving I m suppose to meet Sister Black today; it's Saturday and I need to run to the shopping center just to pick up a few things before I meet Sister Black.

Okay, that's right I need to meet Brother Brown for lunch after I find a pair of shoes. Let me head over to this other store called Your Town and My Shoes. I know that it's going to be a minute when I get there in order for me to find the right shoes, than, hurry over to meet Brother Brown. Hi Sister Black, hi Brother Brown have you been waiting long, no Sister Black I just walked in.

So brother Brown; what are we eating? Whatever there is on the menu. Now, brother Brown you're looking over here at me cross eye, so you better straighten your eyes out. Because, everything over here are off limited until we are legally married; then I am yours, boy.

Yeah, I really love you Sister Black and I am trying to keep it together for me and you, but you look so good over there, just one little bit. Just give me a kiss okay baby here goes, Brother Brown lean over and kiss me. Oh, what: why girl that's your hand?

Brother Brown, you must follow Christ, and even though we want each other, we must do it right this time.

Now, Brother Brown when your in Christ he will help you with your, attitude and our sex drive, each day.

I must be honest Sister Black I want you so bad, it is so difficult sitting here looking at you, just wanting to hold you, just stop right now Brother Brown. I am trying to keep it together too, so don't talk that way to me. I want to just pull you; okay, we just allowed ourselves to get cared away in our lust for each other.

You heard what Sister Walker said, that you must turn over things, and I need to turn over things to God also. Sister Walker and Sister Grace said, we must go over the scripture that the Pastor shared with us. We must truly stay in God's Word so that I will not put our marriage under, because I am a female and want to some time develop an attitude; but I must turn everything over to God.

Yes, your right Sister Black, I must remain in God's present at all times too, to have the patient for you and everything on you that I touch is my. I just want to be in love with you good or when there are hard times, but we can make it Sister Black through our faith in Christ Jesus.

Well, let's placed our food order before we forget why we even came here. This was a nice lunch and we are going to be doing more lunch's as we continue to make time for one another. Brother Brown I will see you in church tomorrow morning. Okay Sister Black I'll see you then.

Deacon Grace and Sister Grace had a feeling about more things to do, Sister Grace are you ready to eat, yes, I'll go in to put something together quick, Paul. Okay Diane, I'll tell the children, their almost finished with the mulch around the trees and the flowers bed. Hey dad! are we going to eat something, Michael said, yes, it will be ready in a few minutes, your mother is putting something together right now.

All right everybody, everyone come in to eat, all right, Franklin and Michael go wash your hand boys. Paul, once everyone is seated will you please bless the food? We sat at the table dad blessed the food and we started eating. Dad or mother do you have any ideal of what the Pastor sermon will be about; No, but I am sure we will learn something from his sermon. It's been a long day Paul and I m little sore, but I feel that a hot bath Will take care of this and I will feel great again. You may be right Diane a nice hot bath, that would do it for me also. Okay, Paul I caught your hint. We can take a bath together, just make sure you wash my back Paul and than I will wash your back, okay honey.

Okay, everyone it's time to get up for church it's Sunday, morning let's get moving, everyone appeared to be just a little slower than any other day of the week, but we made it to church on time. Hi Beth, dad and mother, I am going to sit with Beth, is that okay, yes, Jerry that's find. Jerry we'll see you in the fellowship hall after church.

Okay, mother. You know, Beth that was real nice the kissing, Friday night, but.

I knew you were right Jerry, so let me try to focus on college, I said that so easy Jerry, when I just want you. Okay Beth one thing I do know; God, we must prayer to him to help us to control our emotion. He can help us be safe, Beth. Okay Jerry, I think I need God, more than you do right now, because I am really thinking with my fountain and not my head. Let's prayer Jerry; Beth, Lord keep us, help us, especially me Lord, Beth: I am putting pressure on Jerry to have sex with me, help us so that you will strengthen us, until we do get married in Jesus Name. Amen! Amen!

Beth let's go inside of the church and sat in the same area as we do each Sunday. Jerry, just listen to the chore singing, they sound really great today. Then the Pastor stood up; good morning church it is good to be here: Hallelujah! Hallelujah! Let's give the Lord some praise, everyone applaud all right.

It is time for the Word of God. Let us prayer "Most holy and almighty and wise God we thank you for another day. We thank you for watching over us last night and watching those in the hospital, those that are home and in the convalescent home. Bless everyone that was able to make it out to day to worship, bless your word Lord. In Jesus name we pray. Amen, Amen and Amen."

I will be reading from: "I Corinthian 11:1-9 Be ye followers of me, even as I also am of Christ. Now I praise you, brethren, that ye remember me in all things, And keep the ordinances, as I delivered them to you. But I would have you to know that the head of every man is Christ; and the head of the woman is the man; and the head of Christ is God.

Every man praying or prophesying, having his head covered, dishonor his head. But every woman that prayer or prophesith with her head uncovered dishonor her head: for that is even all one as if she were shaven.

For if the woman is not covered, let her also be shorn: but if it is a shame for a woman to be shorn or shaven, let her be covered. For a man indeed ought not to cover his head, for as much as he is the image and glory of God: but the woman is the glory of the man.

For the man is not of the woman; but the woman of the man. Neither was the man created for the woman; but the woman for the man."

My them: Examine Yourself;

St. Paul begins with commendation of what was praise worthy. When we reprove what is amiss in any, it is very proper to commend what is good in them, it shows the reproof is not from ill-will, and a humor to find fault, it will therefore procure the more regard we have.

Examine Yourself:

In the abound of spiritual gifts bestowed on the Corinthians, it seems that several women had been endowed with the spirit of prophecy, which enabled them to offer prayers for the congregation, or even to give instructions.

Examine Yourself:

However, some abuses had crept in, and the apostle would have them understand that Christ was the immediate Head or Ruler of every man among them: whose honor was concerned in every part of their conduct; and that the man was the immediate head and ruler of the woman.

To whose authority God had subjected her, and who would be disgraced by any impropriety in her behavior.

Examine Yourself:

He also showed that Christ, as Mediator, was subject to the Father. As Christ did the will, and sought the honor of God, so the Christian should avow his subjection to Christ, doing his will and seeking his glory; and the woman should acknowledge her subjection to the man, doing what was honorable to him.

To know our duty in various particulars we should study our relation to God and to each other.

Examine yourself so that God can use you.

He (Paul) reprehends (or blame) the woman's praying or prophesying uncovered, or the man's doing this covered.

It was a mark or token of subjection, for persons to be veiled, or covered, in the eastern countries, contrary to the custom of others, where being covered be tokens superiority and dominion. From this we may then better understand the reason on which this reprehension is grounded.

Examine, examine yourself:

1)The man that prays or prophesies with his head covered, dishonor his Head, that is, Christ, by appearing unsuitable to the rank in which God has placed him. Therefore, we should avoid even in our dress and habit any thing that dishonor Christ.

The women, on the other hand, who prays or prophesies with the head uncovered, dishonor her head, that is, the man. She appears in the dress of her superior, and throws off the token of her subjection, which was the fault of these prophetesses at Corinthian.

The order, in which Divine Wisdom places persons and things, is best and fittest.

Examine Yourself:

2)Another reason was, that the man is the representative of the glorious dominion of God over the world, and the woman shone with reflection of his glory, being made superior to the other creatures here below, but in subjection to her husband, deriving that honor from him out of whom she was made.

Examine Yourself:

3)The women were naturally made subject to man, because she was made for his help and comfort. And she should do nothing, in Christian assemblies, which looked like a claim of equality.

Examine, examine, and examine yourself:

4) She ought to have power on her head, because of the angels. Power, that is, a veil, the token not of her having power or superiority, but of her being under the power of her husband, and subjected to him. If you read the book of "St. Matthews 26:20-29 this is what it said; Now when the even was come, he sat down with the twelve. And as they did eat, he said, Verily I say unto you, that one of you shall betray me. And they were exceeding sorrowful, and began every one of them to say unto him, Lord, is it I? And he answered and said, He that dippeth his hand with me in the dish, the same shall betray me.

The Son of man goeth as it is written of him. But woe unto that man by whom the Son of man is betrayed! It had been good for that man if he had not been born. Then Judas, which betrayed him, answered and said, Master, is it I? He said unto him, Thou hast said.

And as they were eating, Jesus took bread, and blessed it, and broke it, and gave it to the disciples, and said, take, eat; this is my body. And he took the cup, and gave thanks, and gave it to them, saying, Drink yea all of it; For this is my blood of the New Testament; which is shed for many for the remission of sins. But I say unto you, I will not drink henceforth of this fruit of the vine, until that day when I drink it new with you in my Father's kingdom."

Examine, examine yourself: Because, one day God will examine us and see that we are doomed. But, because He loves us so, that he sent His only begotten Son. He was born and walked on this earth for thirty three years; He started to heal people, rise Lazard from the dead, heal the women with the issues of blood, gave the blind sight, and had the lame to walk.

Then the high priest had Christ crucify. He was place on the cross and He cried out to His Father, Father forgave them for they know not what they are doing. He hangs his head and die. On the third day, on the third Day. He got up, and stood on the land and the sea and said, I have all power that's been given unto me: Oh Lord! Oh Lord! He lives and Christ should live in you. Examine yourself and repent for your sins. The doors of the church are open, is there one today for baptism, with Christian experience or is there one by letter. Is their one today?

Deacon Grace look at Sister Grace, man the Pastor preached a dynamite message today I just hope other understood that we all need to examine ourselves and repent for our sins. Yes, Paul did you also heard what the Pastor said about the women being prophetesses, yes, because they were made for the man help, and comfort.

What do you thing Paul, because a lot of the women and men do not attend bible class? You're right Diane; well maybe this will have them come to bible class just to discuss this issue. You know Diane we all want the word tough and preached to us, we just don't want the word to tell us we can no longer do it the way that we are doing it.

Yea, they finger that the bible should be able to justify the things they are doing their way; in order for them to make it into heaven. Well let's go and get children and head for home. There are always people that feel they don't need God and there are people that feel that I can live by the New Testament and others that are feeling they can live by the Old Testament.

When we need to be living by the entire bible all sixty-six books.

Because, when the bible was written, you might feel that the times are difference then the times that we are living in now. Therefore, how much of the bible can be applied correctly to me? The Jews still live by the laws of Moses, but they do not still stone people because of their sins.

They punish the person or people in other ways. I know that this is real hard for women of today to not become ministers, because they said, that God called them to the ministry.

The scripture that the women use, that have inspired them they should do works of charity and benevolence, modest, and consistent deportment, instructing the young and ignorant of their own sex, by writing, by promoting religious and charitable institutions, and by works and offices of piety among themselves.

Christianity places them in their proper sphere; it deprives them of no opportunity for exerting their peculiar talents, or of using their influence to the greatest advantage.

So, women are equal to men, and are in the ministry like men. If there are problems them the women should go to God to find the type of charity work they can do.

But it is for us to be true to ourselves about the relationship we have with God, what dose the bible tell us, God Word dose not lie. So we know that God loves families and he wants men to lead their families and not the women. Knowing that there are single women with children, a head of their household because the man did not step up to his responsibility.

Remember man is in the image of Christ and women represent the church. Oh, man, this has been a beautiful day I don't know the number of people that jointed the church, but it looked like thirty or more people.

Can you thank about it Diane: people that are gray and lesbian must understand this in "Genesis 1:28. And God blessed them, and God said unto them, be fruitful, and multiply, and replenish the earth, and subdue it: and have dominion over the fish of the sea, and over the fowl of the air, and over every living thing that moves upon the earth."

I know sin is easy, also when you think about sin, it is hard to give it up; because you think that it is okay and good; before the eyes of God, because if He didn't want me doing any wrong, them God would have stop me.

But, God stop us every day or tells us every day, that we are wrong or what we are thinking is not of Him: but we do not believe that what we are doing is wrong until something goes wrong or get worst.

How we think to analyze, what we are trying; to have work in our favor, without any though how this will put us under the will of Satan, is wrong. Our children are a blessing for us and we need to protect them from evil things as long as we can do it.

Yes, Paul I agree with you I had to learn by you telling me, how I have sin in our bedroom. And that had a major impact on the other things that made me a church going sinner. I heard that women are to submit and obey their husband, but I told myself that I was not obeying you, Paul, to be your puppet.

But once I study the word I founded out that I was not truly in line with God's Word: because God is the head have Christ, Christ is the head of man, and man is the head of the woman.

And that was knowledge for me. So as I study the bible, I better understood that by trying; to put myself equal with you, Paul, made me compete with you, when you never though about competing with me.

I finger because I am the women that I knew what to do better than you. I didn't call it that word, I wanted to control the children, you, people, and things; I felt that, that was my mission. But I leaned that my mission was to submit and service God; and to submit to you, obey you, and take care of our children, and help out people if I could.

I was always upset with you over something stupid that had nothing to do with you at all: which, had very little to do with me showing you how much I love you daily. Christ showed His love; that is what I learned, and with Christ's love it is shared with your husband, children and others daily.

Paul if my comfort is not present that's, because you would have rejected me. It will never be said again that Diane did not want her husband, because of a bad day. That is the reason we believe in God, so that our bad days, can become good ones; from our faith and our prayers to God.

Diane, your right, and now with all that you have said, which is good information to share with the young girls like Beth, Susan, Jane, and with the ladies gathering.

That's right Paul, this is what I am going to do is call some of the other sisters and work on an outline to teach our young ladies. Okay children come on and eat, before the food gets cold. Diane, as we look at the roles for men and women as it is pointed out in the bible; it should be a discussion even if the women will have a major problem with it.

One other thing that is also very important is that the men need a class just to discuss their role in the family as head of household. Now, what the bible is telling you: if your husband is a godly man, than the wife would receive more respect and loved. If he is not a godly man, than you're going to have it a little harder than some other wives. But in either case, the bible did not put the women over the man.

You know Paul, I guess, Pastor Johnson will teach on this subject on Monday, night bible class on marriage. Because; I learned when the husband or wife is disrespectful to the other spouse, just to raise themselves up this is against God's Word.

Therefore, how important is it that we are making sure that God's Word mean more to us then just reading and not studying it. It must change our ways in order that it is affective in life that we understand; what our relationship, is all about with God.

This is all ways a good time for families to start off the work, week with God, and realize the education that comes with it. As the families get up each day and prepare for work and school we should understand, with our education, the week shell begin. It was Monday and we had to get going to work and to school. Knowing that this evening, we will be attending bible class.

I was really rushing you Paul, to get to bible class tonight; because I wanted you to hear the comments that some of the other members were making. Okay, Jerry, Michael, Pauline and Franklin; make sure that everyone wait, for the other one before leaving the building going to the parking lot. Brother Harris wills you lead us in pray. Okay, Pastor. Most holy and wise God, thank you for this day and our travel to work and to bible class. Help us to understand your word and each other in Jesus name Amend! Amend! And Amend.

Okay, last week in bible class we kind of stopped with Sister Black talking. Sister Black did you want to say something else. Ah, yes, Pastor: Well, I think everyone knows that Brother Brown and I, are getting married in six months and the Pastor, I know we will be receiving counseling.

But, after hearing all these sisters talk about how they close down making love in their marriage, what do I have to look forward too? Because nine out of ten women have close down and maybe one man out of fifty may have stop making love to his wife.

Are we so selfish that we are untruthful to our husband or wife and yet, we say that God is in us?

Pastor, yes, Sister Small, can I tell Sister Black this much; Okay, Sister Small, you are starting out with the Word of God, keep studying the word so He will give you the strength; you will need to pull your marriage through; what every comes your way.

Be a helpmate from the start and make it your job to love God and your husband. Keeping this up every day, even when it gets tough. And Brother Brown, keep Sister Black in prayer, because as you and her are going to hit some small and big bump along the way.

Yes, thank you Sister Small, Pastor, yes, Sister Johnson. I didn't have a chance to respond to what Pastor said on last week, but I wanted to correct some of the things that the Pastor did say. The bottom line was that I was real selfish to the Pastor and I am really a shame of that because I was always in the church building my entire life.

Sisters and brothers; please don't just come to the church building like I did for so many years; but study God's Word for yourself, so that it lives in you. There is no doubt that as I service God daily that heaven is truly my home.

Now the sermon on Sunday talks about men and women, so the men need not take a back seat on the Word of God.

You need to live it every day in all that you do; women need to listen to their husbands; trying to tell then what they should be doing. Women you want to tell you husband what to do; how much of what your husbands have told you to do, have you actually done?

You see the controlling just did not start in the bedroom, but that's the way she is acting in all the things that she doses. Sometime the wife just needed to sit down and not say one word about anything to be done, until she can think through the issues, on how she is able to do it, just in case the husband is not able to do this task.

Because if your husband told you things to do every time you turn around then you will say, that he is trying to control you. You, think. Women stop trying to be the boss and God gave you a position, to be the helpmate as it is stated in the scriptures.

We have had a great marital bible class that we should draw on daily from the scriptures to apply them to our life. Now I know some of you sisters are thinking how come, nothing was said about the men not following God: are there any brothers that are willing to share their experiences. Okay, I see Brother Apple, Brother Small, Brother Harold and Brother little.

Okay brothers what is it that you want to share with the sisters? Well, Pastor, I was not willing to come to God because I finger that I had enough God in me, just because I went to the church building, as Sister Johnson put it.

Not that I was running around on my wife, I would just make it hard for us to agree on things. She would tell me, if you want this marriage to work you need to start reading God's Word.

I understood from studying the word, I was the head of the house; and kind of knew what my responsibility where as the husband. The responsibility rested on the husband shoulders how he treated his wife, children, and others. Because men are in the image of God, then we are expected to be loving, kind, respectful to our wife and children, and suffer through things that our wife and children may do. You had to be in prayer always even when you didn't feel like it, because of the things that happens to the husband he must be humble in order not to be so easily anger. Okay, Brother Small, and the other brothers, the word it always told the men what their responsibility where when it comes to life and the wife, children and others. But, Pastor, yes Brother Harold, I did the opposite, of everything that was shared in these few bible class discussion. My wife Sister Harold will tell you that I ran around on her for years. I really can't blame my wife, because it was my problem, for the reason I did what I did? If I said anything else it would not be true. I was not saved and I just ran after the women. I thank God for my wife, because she prayed for me all the time. She had plans of leaving me a long time ago, but I begged her to stay and give me another chance. A year ago, I blew it and she left with the children. I called her an apologize, and week talked for a few weeks and she told me that I need to come to the Lord; that would be the only way that she will come back to me. So saints here I am, a member of this church have saved me and help my marriage where we are talking about moving back together next week. Pastor's, knows what have been going on with my family since I joint the church over a year ago, but how things are and now how things are going to be. Well, Pastor, Brother Apple, this is a little hard for me because I have been under the weather for a period of time and I could not make love to my wife and she would be upset about that; and I didn't understand why she would feel that way. One day she said Fed, I know it is a problem for you, and other times I would tell her no just because I wanted to. But, now because of the illness and I just want to hold you and make love to you, but I can't, because your sick and I am just hot for you now. So I don't know how long it will be for me to get well but with our prayers God will make away. Thank you, Pastor.

Chapter 15

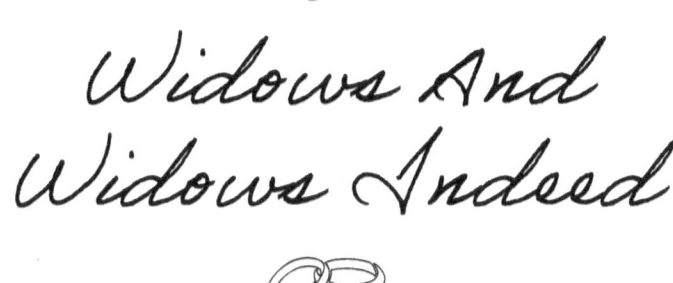

Widows And Widows Indeed

Let us look at "Isaiah 2:3-5 They shall also be a crown of glory in the hand of the Lord, and a royal Diadem in the hand of thy God. They shall no more be termed forsaken; neither shall thy land any more be termed desolate: but thou shalt be called Heph'zi-bah, and thy land Ben'-lah: for the Lord delighteth in thee, and thy land shall be married.

For as a young man marrieth a virgin, so shall thy sons marry thee: and as the bridegroom rejoiceth over the bride, so shall thy God rejoice over thee."

"St. Matthew 19:7-9 They say unto him, why did Moses then command to give a writing of divorcement, and to put her away? He said unto them, Moses because of the hardness of your hearts suffered you to put away your wives: but from the beginning it was not so.

And I say unto you, Whosoever shall put away his wife, except it be for fornication, and shall marry another, committeth adultery: and whoso marrieth her which is put away doth commit adultery." "St. Luke 16:15-18 And he said unto them, ye are they which justify yourselves before men: but God knoweth your hearts; for that which is highly esteemed among men is abomination in the sight of God.

The Law and the prophets were until John: since that time the kingdom of God is preached, and every man presseth into it. And it is easier for heaven and earth to pass, than one tittle of the Law to fail. Whosoever put away his wife, and marrieth another, committeth adultery: and whosoever marrieth her that is put away from her husband committeth adultery."

Brother Brown, the Mosesic Law for divorce was set up, because of the compliance that men had about their wives. If things not done around the house, in the house, the children were not good, or the wife could not or would not have his children. If someone saw her leaving from another man home, did not want to make love, but every once in awhile.

Whatever the reason men give, letters of divorce and married another woman they felt, was the type of women they wanted. The scriptures had to be understood; so that they would not be uncommitted to their wives. You also, heard what Jesus said, regarding divorce that it was not to be so, from the beginning.

Christ, is saying, you should understand the scripture, first, and be committed to Him, men and women, when there are problems larger or small, as they both come to God, He will resolve their problems for them.

God, will allow you to be in the mind of Joseph, the eleven son of Jacob, as Joseph interpret Pharaoh dreams of the cows and wheat. You are also, to store up, when things are going well, so when it is hard times, you have save up, stored up, supplies to help you through the difficult times with every problem (this is also prayer time).

For this planing, to work you need to be in Christ Jesus, not only for your salvation but also for your finance. To have supplies for your family in time of need, as your love will play a role in the planing, so there are no unjust argument over money, allowing you to speak the truth, about the finances.

Your body, is the Lord's, and before God, He allowed your spouse to have your body and the money. God blessed you both with His giving according to Christ's blessing. Whatever is yours, love your spouse and be kind to your spouse, to have the best relationship possible, because they are yours forever.

Now, we have talked about divorce, but what we have not talked about, is a widow or widow indeed. If you will turn to "I Timothy 5:1-16 Rebuke not an elder, but in treat him as a father; and the younger men as brethren: The elder women as mother; the younger women as sister, with all purity. Honor widows that are widows indeed.

But if any widow have children or nephews, let them learn first to show, pity at home and to reunite their parents. For that is good and acceptable before God now she that is a widow indeed, and desolate, trust in God, and continue in supplications and prayers night and day. But she that live, in pleasure is dead while she live. And these things give in charge, that they may be blameless. But of any provide not for his own, and specially for those of his own, house, he has denied the faith, and is worse than an infidel, let not a widow be taken into the number under threescore years old, having been the wife of one man. Well reported of good works, if she have brought up children, if she have lodged strangers, if she have washed the saints feet, if she have relieved the afflicted, if she have diligently followed every good work.

But the younger widows refuse for when they have begun to wax wanton against Christ, they will marry. Having damnation because they have cast off their first faith. And withal they learn to be idle, wandering about from house to house; and not only idle, but tattlers also and busy bodies, speaking things, which they ought not.

I will therefore that the younger women marry, bear children, guide the house, and give none occasion to the adversary to speak reproachfully. For some are already turned aside after Satan. If any man or woman that believe have widows, let them relieve them, and let not the church be charged; that it may relieve them that are widows indeed."

Okay, Pastor can you break this down for us, yes, Brother Brown, you should respect our older members and look at the older men as a father and the younger men as a brother. That we will look at the older women as mother and the younger women as a sister.

We must, put things, in place while we live, because once we pass, help will be hard to find for our living relatives. We should make sure that what ever we have, that our life insurance policy, should be more than just for the funeral. There should be enough life insurance coverage in our life insurance policy, to cover, all the debt and our social security will help maintain the wife and children life style, if the husband dies.

In many cases today, the wife may need to have a life policy on her to cover the debt, due to, many of the things, that the wife wanted, in the home. Cost of the home, education for the children, medical insurance, ones pension plan and other investments that can be use to maintain the family for life.

Any wills, or other properties, other investment, other life policies, partnerships corporation, coin-collection, antique, paintings, bonds, share options, and mutual funds.

Your wife or husband should be made a where of these opportunities, before or right after the wedding ceremony. Husbands are giving the responsibility to make sure that supplements are made available for their family; god, fore bit, if something should happen to him: the family life style, would be alter slightly. But because, he had set up provision for his family everything should work out all right.

However, there are a number of families, that are not that blessed, to have a husband to be that concern to setup provision for his family before his death. Many families are really destitute and are truly in financial need and have no known church family or family members to turn to. It is so important that the husband and wife are in Christ Jesus, in order that they will do right in the sight of God and for each other for their family.

We are to honor widows that are widows indeed, to maintain them, to help them with respect and tenderness.

But, the church should not be charged, with their maintenance of the widows who had relatives able to maintain them.

This is what family is support to do. If parents, tough their children well the children will take care of there parents in need. And this is acceptable before God. If she is a widow indeed and to be maintained at the charge of the church, she must, trust in God.

Widowhood is a desolate place, but let widows trust in the Lord and rejoice that they have a God to trust. Those who trust in God must continue in prayer, because, if by faith we confide in God, by prayer we give glory to God, and commit ourselves to His guidance.

The Word said Anna was a widow indeed, who served God, with fasting and prayer night and day. She was not a widow indeed that lived in pleasure, a luxurious, self-indulgent life. This type of widow, is dead while she lives, she is not a member of the church, but as a carcass, or a mortified member. If they live in pleasure, they are dead while they live, spiritually dead, dead in trespasses and in sin.

They are in this world, without a purpose, until the end of life. If any husband or wife do not maintain their poor relatives, they deny the faith. For, the design of Christ, was to confirm the law, the fifth commandment of which is, "honor your father and mother". So that those that deny the faith, who disobey the law, they will endure much more, if they provide not for their wives and children, who are parts of them.

It is the indispensable duty, of children and grand children to requite the kindness of their aged parents; and if professors of the gospel. Through selfishness or any corrupt principle, neglect or refuse to provide for they're near parents, they are worse than those who do not profess to believe the doctrines of grace.

Aged widows, and others of good character, left destitute in the decline of life, should be honored as well as supported. This is for the widow who discharged official duties in the church that visited the sick and the poor females, and attended to various matters connected with ministers and strangers.

This is some of the work done by proper wives. If she have brought up children; if she have been ready to entertain needy Christians and godly ministers, if she have relieved the afflicted when she was able.

The younger widows will be weary of employment in the church, and of living by the rule, as they must do; they will marry and cast off their first faith, (Christ) their engagements to the church to discharge the trust in them.

They might be induced to marry again, and as their entrance into the number of devoted widows implied an engagement to the contrary, so their departure may be look on as a rebellion against Christ.

They learn to be idle, and not only idle but tatters. Being mischief among neighbors, and sow discord among brothers. If women do not mind their business, but are tatters, this will give reason to others to question the faith of them that are Christian.

The younger-widows therefore need to be engage in the duties of married, and the care of a family. Than to be exposed to the temptation of the offices in business, that they would wish that they had not, which give Satan the occasion to test their faith in the gospel.

This may cause widow condemnation, and fidelity to Christ, because they perhaps married an unsaved person that is doing worldly things, and the widow may be expose to condemnation unless she repent. All believers, are required to help such widows, belonging to their families, that are destitute, that the church, are to make sure, that they are not prevented from helping them, that are entirely destitute and friendless.

Now let me give you some more scripture. "Jeremiah 3:2-5 Lift up thine eyes unto the high places, and see where you has not been lien with.

In the ways has you sat for them; as the Arabian in the wilderness; and you has polluted the land with your whoredoms and with your wickedness.

Therefore the showers have been with hold, and there has been no latter rain; and you had a whore's forehead, you refused to be ashamed. Wilt you not from this time cry unto me, my father, you art the guide of my youth? Will he reserve his anger forever? Will he keep it to the end? Behold, you has spoken and done evil things as you could."

Leviticus 21:10-15 "And he that is the high priest among his brethren, upon who so head the anointing oil was poured, and that is consecrated to put on the garments, shall not uncover his head, nor rend his clothes. Neither shall he go into any dead body, nor defile himself for his father, or for his mother.

Neither shall he go out of the sanctuary, nor profane the sanctuary of his God; for the crown of the anointing oil of his God is upon him: I am the Lord.

And he shall take a wife in her virginity. A widow, or a divorced women, or profane, or an harlot, these shall he not take: but he shall take a virgin of his own people to wife. Neither shall he profane his seed among his people: for I the Lord do sanctify him."

Leviticus 22:11-16 "But if the priest buy any soul with his money, he shall eat of it, and he that is born in his house: they shall eat of his meat. If the priest's daughter also be married unto a stranger, she may not eat of an offering of the holy things.

But if the priest's daughter be a widow, or divorced, and have no child, and is returned unto her father's house, as in her youth, she shall eat of her father's meat; but there shall no stranger eat there of.

And if a man eat of the holy thing unwittingly, then he shall put the fifth part there of unto it, and shall give it unto the priest with the holy thing. And they shall not profane the holy thing of the children of Israel, which they offer unto the Lord;

Or suffer them to bear the iniquity of trespass, when they eat their holy things: for I the Lord do sanctify them."

He shell wash his flesh with water, and when the sun is down he shall be clean, and shall afterward eat of the holy things; because it is his food. That no stranger who did not belong to some family of the priests, should eat of the holy things; and if he did it unwittingly, he must make restitution. That the sacrifices offered must be without blemish.

That they must be more than eight days old, and that the sacrifices of thanksgiving must be eaten the same day they were offered. Holy things were the parts of the sacrifices given to the priests; also the shrew bread, and whatever was presented to the Lord. Let us also remember that the Lord requires us to reverence His name, His truths, His ordinances, and commandments.

The man who enters into the ministry out of covetousness or ambition, while he indulges in known, allowed, and habitual sin. As well as those professed Christians who make religion their pretense, but gain their object-such persons, in fact, presume to eat of the holy things with uncleanness upon them, and must answer for it to God. Let us them beware of hypocrisy, and examine us concerning our sinful defilement, seeking to be purified, from them in sin, in the blood of Christ, and by His sanctifying spirit.

Nor can the minister, who loves the souls of the people, suffer them to continue in this dangerous delusion. He must call upon them, not only to repent of their sins, and forsake them; but to put their whole trust in the atonement of Christ, by faith in His name, for pardon and acceptance with God-thus only will the Lord sanctify them for His peculiar people.

Yes, deacon Johnson, is the word telling us that we should be of the same spirit to have that anointing oil put upon us. And, that we should not have anyone before God, and respect God as Lord over us. Yes, Deacon Johnson, that is correct, God is letting us know that if your saying that you are a child of God and your attitude and your spiritual mind does not line up, with God, and then you are doom unless you repent to God.

Now, if, we listen to what Sister Walker, Sister Johnson and Sister Grace stated on how they had to repent for how they treated their husbands with their bodies. That they realized that they where not in God's spirit not just in the treatment of their husbands, but they did not truly have the love of God in their mind, heart and spirit.

Because, as it is stated in this scripture. "St. Matthew 6:33 But seek ye first the kingdom of God, and his righteousness; and all these things shall be added unto you." "Romans 5:1-10 Therefore being justified by faith, we have peace with God through our Lord Jesus Christ:

By whom also we have access by faith into this grace wherein we stand, and rejoice in hope of the glory of God. And not only so, but we glory in tribulations also: knowing that tribulation worketh patience; And patience, experience; and experience, hope:

And hope make not ashamed; because the love of God is shed abroad in our hearts by the Holy Ghosts which is given unto us. For when we were yet without strength, in due time Christ died for the ungodly. For scarcely for a righteous man will one die: yet peradventure for a good man some would even dare to die.

But God commend his love toward us, in that, while we were yet sinners, Christ died for us.

Chapter 16

A Relationship With God

Much more then, being now justified by his blood, we shall be saved from wrath through him. For if. When we were enemies, we were reconciled to God by the death of his Son, much more, being reconciled, we shall be saved by His life."

"I Corinthian 7:4-5 The wife has not power of her own body, but the husband: and likewise also the husband hath not power of his own body, but the wife. Defraud you not one the other, except it be with consent for a time, that ye may give yourselves to fasting and prayer; and come together again, that Satan tempt you not for your in continency."

You see, the sin is not that you are not making love with your husband, or wife, but you allow other sinful things to enter your mind, and your spirit. Other, so, call Christians that have corrupted your spirit, and now your love, of God is gone and the spirit of Satan, is in you.

So, now any advances that your husband or wife will make to you, should not lead to rejection, and turn into disagreements, into many things, that are not of God and love is not displaced.

But, what we need: is to have faith in God, through Jesus Christ, to help us with all things; that are happening, in our life, in order to strengthen our belief, that God will bring us out of this situation.

We must justify our faith by our reliance on God for everything in order to build our relationship with Him. Here are some things that we need to consider.

Have we went so far with our disrespect that we are blaming our spouse for every little thing to continual making ourselves feel good?

We should be glad and happy about all things that God has blessed us with; He touch us this morning, the husband, the wife and the children are well.

Your brothers and sisters are doing find, so what are you really upset about, these things that may be troubling you are not going to keep you from dying with it.

We have too, much to be joyous about, to be unhappy, God has blessed you and your family and all you can do is point fingers at your spouse about something they have done accidentally.

What about the things you have done accidentally or purposely? Don't you want your spouse to forgive you or over look this issue?

Where is your forgiveness, you can only forgive, if God love is in you. Or is Satan, still resident in you, Repent, to receive God my brother and sister, Repent, to enjoy the glory of God, for His blessing to be upon you.

Pastor, what else can really be said, about relationships. There are these points that must be consider at all time:

We do like to critic, attacking your spouse. If we are feeling contempt, tear down, or rolling your eye sand play it off as humor. When you are defensiveness it is because your reasoning or excuses no longer work for you. When you shut down it dose not help the relationship if you are not talking about the problems or issues that you have?

Conflict can be destructive to the relationship.

All couples will engage in these types of behaviors at some point in their relationship, but learn how to navigate through them to receive the core source of the problem.

If your center point for each other is the other spouse, then you would fine, that your love and joy is elevated, because, you are a where of who is the center of your love. If you and your spouse served each other and love God, which would have joy in you. Your marriage would be beautiful and you would be in the hands of God. With God in the center of your marriage you can better understand your love for one another. Our worship to God would increase our service to Him and bring our marriage back to God.

We must understand that you were not sinning because, you did not make love with your spouse, but your lack of faith in God, cause you to sin.

You just added sex issues to your sin list. Keeping, love making, from your spouse, because now you are really in the Lord or having the mind set that making love is beneath you, or blaming the other spouse, just to say no to love making, dose not help your relationship with your spouse.

Remember "Hebrews 13:4 Marriage is honorable in all, and the bed undefiled: but whoremongers and adulteress God will judge."

Divorce in the church is at a rate of fifty percent, as it is for non-believers in the world. The same problems Exists, between husbands and wives, exist inside and outside of the church. Some one in the marriage does not want to make love. When you come to God and understand your responsibility as a husband and a wife: you know that making love will be in the marriage, and no one person has the right, to control, when you will make love.

We want to stamp out all sin, but we have not address the gift that God has given only to the husband and wives (male and female only), the gift of pleasure and children. This union is blessed by God, to give you pleasure and children, and it, should keep on giving you pleasure, after the children are no longer coming forth.

People, are wanting to get married, because they want to be with this women or man for the rest of their life; because the man makes that women feels good she laugh, smiles, he is kind, loving, respectful and caring. The women make this man feel good he laugh, smiles, she is kind, loving, respectful and caring.

Many times at this point in dating, sex should not be an issues, because he is not yours, and you are not his, to do; what you will? We must preserve the gift for the wedding night. We did not want to fornicate, before we are married. Because the man and the woman; need to know that his body belongs to the wife and the wife body belongs to the husband: When they married and not until that time.

It is so important that we commit to God, and to each other; that we love God and will live by His Word. To direct our life through our studying: of the word that we learn how to love our wife and our husband (male and female couples only); dearly and truthfully without lies. We must learn that you are with your wife according to knowledge through the scripture,

That we must sanctify ourselves (the male husband for the female wife) for our spouse (one man and one Woman only).

Do not be a fornicator appointed to death.

"I Corinthians 5:3-13 For I verily, as absent in body, but present in spirit, have judged already, as though I were present, concerning him that hath so done this deed, In the name of our Lord Jesus Christ, when ye are gather together, and my spirit, with the power of our Lord Jesus Christ,

To deliver such an one unto Satan for the destruction of the flesh, that the spirit may be saved in the day of the Lord Jesus. Your glorying is not good. Know ye not that a little leaven, leaven the whole Lump? Purge out therefore the old leaven, that ye may be a new lump, as ye are unleavened, For even Christ out Passover is sacrificed for us:

Therefore let us keep the feast, not with old leaven, neither with the leaven of malice and wickedness; but with the unleavened bread of sincerity and truth. I wrote unto you in an epistle not to company with fornicators: Yet not altogether with the fornicators of this world, or with the covetous, or extortioners, or with idolaters; for then must ye needs go out of the world.

But now I have written unto you not to keep company, if any man that is called a brother be a fornicator, or covetous, or an idolater, or a railer, or a drunkard, or an extortioner; with such an one no not to eat. For what have I to do to judge them also that are without? Do not ye judge them that are within? But them that are without God judgeth. Therefore put away from among yourselves that wicked person."

You know Pastor; this has been blow by blow of what was needed in this church, because we must get this message out to the community to let them know that God is for you and your marriage. Well thank, Sister Grace and Sister Walker: Pastor, I wish I felt like this many years ago; when I first got married, because I know that Deacon Walker would have enjoyed the marriage much better, and I would have also.

Pastor, you are right Sister Walker, because Deacon Grace and I talked earlier in our marriage, he wanted to know what my problems where? It took awhile, but thanks be to God, the Lord help me to understand, what love truly means and that His Word is true. You're right Sister Walker and

Sister Grace, if more people will be truthful in their marriage and spent more time loving, you would reduce divorce in the churches.

Deacon William, will you let us in prayer, "Most holy and heavenly Father we thank you for this evening bible class and prayer that everyone will make it home safely. And we thank you Lord for our Pastor that you watch over him and his family as we look to you for all time and things, as we depart from this place, but not from your present in your Son Jesus name. Amen! Amen!"

Okay, Pastor, Sister Walker I'll see you both if it the Lord will next week for bible class, oh, not Sunday, oh, yes, Pastor, see you Sunday. Oh, Paul, yes Diane where are you going, I was just going to make sure that the children where on their way to the car. Okay, but do me a favor, just come over to me and hold me you beast. Oh, Paul, remember we are in the church parking lot so don't get carry away with your kissing and holding me.

Ah, Diane, I just love you, okay Paul, we will pick it up when we get home, the children are on their way to the car. Okay, guys, let go home, so we can get up for work and school. Well dad and mother, Beth and I are going to the University of Connecticut and we can commute from home. Jerry that will mean you will need a car. AH, yes, I wanted to talk to you and mother about that I know it's a change in plans.

Yes, it is, Jerry, and I have no ideal what the insurance cost will be for you. Well, dad I will have a job, so I will be able to pay for the monthly car payment, Insurance, repair and put gas in the car.

I applied at this insurance company for a pre-law inter-ship, I should know if I have that position by this Friday. Okay, Jerry, let your mother and I look into this car for you and we will see what, we can do, by Friday, how much we can help you out, okay, dad.

Okay every one we are at home; wake Franklin up, Jerry and let him walk in the house. Oh, Franklin, you got to get up for school tomorrow, it's school time. No Franklin, just getup and go into the house so that you can get into bed for school tomorrow. Also, Paul, don't forget, to lock up, and make your way up stair to the bedroom: so you can finish what you started. Oh, what I started! As I re-call you called me over to you Diane.

Paul, I know, I just wanted you to take care of our stuff that was stopped in the church parking lot. The children may have a snack in their bedroom and we are in the honeymoon suite, so bring it on boy. The wife should feel safe and not cheap with her husband at no time in their marriage, there in the bride chamber.

There are many difference type of challenges, that our children will be faces with, in their life. And the largest, of them all, is who will they married? John and Jane wanted to be married. Because they where very much in love with each other. John spoke to Jane's mother about getting married, and her mother said, that would be find with her, as long as they complete college.

John and Jane wanted the wedding by July, but Jane mother talked John and Jane into September, of the next year. Jane's mother said she really wanted to see how the two of us work together. So she said, plan your wedding. Oh, boy this is going to be fun John, planing our wedding. Just you wait and see John. Jane you're jumping for joy, I am glad that we are doing this with time on our side.

Jane we need to talk with my parents, as well and share this information about us getting married. Okay, hi dad and mother Jane and I have something to tell you; it's about us getting married. What are your thoughts? John's father and mother were not that happy, but they said, we knew that John had stated a couple of years ago, that, when he graduated from high school that he wanted to married you Jane. John had you and Jane discussed this with Jane's mother yet? Yes, dad, we have and just left from over her house. Jane's mother wanted us to wait until next September to get married. That would give us plenty of time to plan to wedding as we attend college. So I guess, because of John's new computer chip, that he develop and this computer company purchase the chip, from John, this will give you and Jane the start that you will need.

John, you and Jane are still going to the University of Connecticut right. Yes, dad, in the fall. I know that it is going to be hard being married and going to college, but I feel that this is the only way that I would be able to enjoy my life with Jane. Okay, so the two of you are starting to plan this wedding. All right, let me know if you need some help, John.

Bob and Susan are still working on other thing to build up their relationship with each other. Susan, how come you don't want to get married to me. Do you think what you did at the move theater has dropped out of my head; Bob? No. Well, I need to make sure that you are not going to act like that, with me ever again, Bob.

Susan, I know we've been seeing each other for four years now. But, Susan, will you married me, Susan blush and cover her face and cried. Bob, you know we need to wait; do I need to give you an answer right now? Not right now, but soon. Bob I want to be with you, but I need to speak to my parents and you need to speak to your parents, okay. Yea, your right Susan I will. Bob kiss Susan and left for home.

Single people want to be married and really don't have a clue about; what they are planning to commit to? When you married there is no more privacy, no more my stuff: It is now our stuff, the bathroom is no longer private it is now public, your body he can pull on you and you can pull on him. You have control of her body and she has control of your body.

You are to share everything, with each other; and love doing it: because you are supposes to have this unconditional love for each other. That is what Sister Black and Brother Brown was able to get out of the bible class discussion for the past; two month.

They have setup a time for pre-marital counseling with Pastor Johnson. When you stay in love, God's Word is love, and your, marriage will work like a well oil machine. Your love will reduce selfishness, and anger to your marriage relationship, with God keeping sin away from your spirit. That is the reason you must go to God every day to remain in love, with Him, so your spouse can be the benefactor, of your relationship with God, your love will be stronger and true with your spouse.

And, we know there have been many problems in our marriage, but we remain in love, with God your marriage will survive every storm. When the love drops, that means you put God and His Word down. That means you have open up yourself to problem, that you will not be able to bear. Sin, is invited into your life by you; because you no longer have time for anyone. You are feeling that you need more out of life then just being married to this person (Husband or wife) for the rest of your life.

Marriage is taken up, to, much of my time, so let me find someone else that I do not need to be married to, where I can spent my time with him or her and not be pull down with their issues, that are drowning me. By moving our focus from God to ourselves we destroy our marriage. Your faith in God and your believe keeps peace, love, kindness, caring, respect and joy in your marital life not just for you, but for the whole marriage husband and wife.

Under God's doctrine you have a life time partner to direct you, teach you; what love means and how it feels, how thing are worked out in your behave, because of your relationship with God. God give us these wonderful blessing to enjoy and to be bountiful in our life, so much so, that He wants us to enjoy this life with that beautiful women and that handsome man. And because God said, "It is not good that man should be alone-Genesis 2:18" we did not have anyone that was our equal.

So God created woman for man that she will bear his children and is his helpmate and comfort the man, as he needed to be comforted. They made love in the garden no restriction to each other. The husband and wife scarify, themselves, for each other to do the following for their relationship. Intimacy, children, homes, home decoration, dinner parties, children activities, being patient to each other and all of this should be done in LOVE.

As we conclude The Serendipity of Marriage, please Remember when the husband and wife are untrue, and there are lies, and disrespect what are you planing to get out of this type of relationship? Truly even one that is in Christ, there will be problems in their marriage that will create pressure on the relationship.

We must remember that as we prayer and study God's Word.

It should bring us to a clear mind to think about the, Words of God, which has been study about marriage. That we should be ready to ask one another forgiveness; because of the words that have been passed between us: knowingly, that how things happen had a difference of opinion, in the meaning of our words.

In so many ways we are blessed; but still we hold on to things that have lesser important than our relationship with God, and our spouse. Thinking that you know some thing on your spouse because of these negative views you have. We all want God's gifts, but how many of us want the gift of God? Love is a gift from God; kindness is a gift from God; heartache is a gift from God; sorrow is a gift from God; enjoyment, happiness, fun, caring, being in a sound mind, doing the right things, living the godly way, are all gifts from God.

The question is how do we receive, these, gifts? Gifts, can be obtain by having faith and believing in God and repentance; however you must gain experience with God to improve your faith and have a prayer line by going through trial and tribulations. Servicing God is what you must do, single or married, replenishing the earth is done rightly if you're married. If you choose not to do God service or get married then you will be outside of the will of God.

God makes us to worship him and gave us the ability to create others like us in order that they will also service God. Train, up a child learning about God. We, as people are no better, than the next person, and it does not matter what race you are you must believe in God.

Many people are better off financially and have a lot of material items; but their favor can be good or bad with God. The people that are following Christ understand that they must submit themselves to God, then they know the love of God.

Their, love of God, will help them to understand how to love others. As we learn about God from are studies, prayer, faith, our joy and happiness will shall reach higher heights that are out of this world, because you are looking at the kingdom of God, world of joy, happiness and love. All the money in the world cannot replace your love and you can not buy the love that you need.

There will not be, anything that you will not do, for someone, that you truly are in love with. If you or our parents would just take us in their arms and firmly bring us to understand more about God, you will find what a beautiful thing it will be.

Therefore, marriage should be about love, if your marriage, is based on, any other reason and are truly not in Christ, love will not be displayed in the relationship. When husbands and wives are truly in Christ the problems that they will have would be handle by the three of them (Jesus, Husband and The Wife). He will give them strength and forgive them, as they work out their problems of forgiveness to each other.

They will not allow anything to put their marriage under. The other women, the other man, money, and children. They understand their wedding vows, and they are studying God's Word and they will repent for their attitude and selfishness to each other before God.

They will not make excuses to their husband or wife about their duties to one another. Christ must be in the center of your life in order that He is in the center of your marriage. Don't blame your wife for your problems and don't blame your husband for your problems.

Just blame yourself for not being truly in Christ Jesus and that is the reason, why things are not working, the way it should with you knowing God, in your life or in your marriage. Lies, disrespect, unkindness, unhappiness, no joy, no peace, no family, no friend, no romance, no love, and no intimacy, and no love making; because you do not have the God you desire in you.

Remember Jesus Christ is our Lord and Savior. God Bless.

REFERENCE PAGE

King James Bible–KJV